EXTREME 3-D
OUTER SPACE

BY PAUL BECK

SCHOLASTIC

an imprint of
SCHOLASTIC
www.scholastic.com

Published by Tangerine Press, an imprint of Scholastic Inc.,
557 Broadway, New York, NY 10012

Scholastic Canada Ltd., Markham, Ontario

Scholastic Australia Pty. Ltd, Gosford NSW

Scholastic New Zealand Ltd., Greenmount, Auckland

Grolier International, Inc., Makati City, Philippines

becker&mayer!
BOOK PRODUCERS

Produced by becker&mayer!
11120 NE 33rd Place, Suite 101
Bellevue, WA 98004
www.beckermayer.com

If you have questions or comments about this product, please visit www.beckermayer.com/customerservice and click on Customer Service Request Form.

Edited by Ben Grossblatt
Cover designed by Shane Hartley
Book interior designed by Rosanna Brockley
3-D anaglyph effects by Joe Mentele and Bill Whitaker
Product development by Chris Tanner
Production management by Larry Weiner
Photo research by Zena Chew
All rights reserved.

Photo credits: Cover and title page: All images from NASA. Pages 2-3, background: Veil Nebula © NASA, ESA, and the Hubble Heritage (STScI/AURA)-ESA/Hubble Collaboration. Page 4: Sun © NASA/JPL-Caltech/NRL/GSFC. Page 5: Sun's magnetic field © Hinode, JAXA/NASA; Helix Nebula © NASA, NOAO, ESA, the Hubble Helix Nebula Team, M. Meixner (STScI), and T.A. Rector (NRAO). Pages 4-5, background: Galaxy NGC 1569 © NASA, ESA, the Hubble Heritage Team (STScI/AURA), and A. Aloisi (STScI/ESA). Page 6: MESSENGER photo of Mercury © NASA/Johns Hopkins University Applied Physics Laboratory/Carnegie Institution of Washington. Page 7: Artist's impression of the Mercury Composite Spacecraft, BepiColombo mission © ESA/EADS Astrium; a scarp on Mercury © NASA/Johns Hopkins University Applied Physics Laboratory/Carnegie Institution of Washington. Pages 6-7, background: Milky Way Galaxy © NASA, JPL-Caltech, Susan Stolovy (SSC/Caltech) et al. Page 8: Venus © NASA/JPL. Page 9: Mat Mons © NASA/JPL; Sedna Planitia © NASA/JPL/USGS. Pages 8-9, background: Star AE Aurigae © T.A. Rector and B.A. Wolpa, NOAO, AURA and NSF. Page 10: Moon © NASA/JPL/USGS. Page 11: Copernicus Crater © NASA/JPL/USGS; solar corona © NASA/JPL/USGS. Pages 10-11, background: Red Supergiant Star V838 Monocerotis © NASA, ESA and H.E. Bond (STScI). Page 12: Twin Peaks panorama from Mars Pathfinder © NASA/JPL. Page 13: Dust storm at the north pole of Mars © NASA/JPL/Malin Space Science Systems; Mars rocks © NASA/JPL/Cornell/USGS/Texas A&M. Pages 12-13, background: Galaxy cluster Abell 3627 © X-ray: NASA/CXC/UVa/M. Sun et al; H-alpha; Optical: SOAR/MSU/NOAO/UNC/CNPq-Brazil/M.Sun et al. Page 14: Jupiter © NASA/JPL/Space Science Institute. Page 15: Io © NASA/JPL/University of Arizona; cloud model © NASA/JPL-Caltech. Pages 14-15, background: Supernova remnant E0102 inside the Small Magellanic Cloud © NASA, ESA, the Hubble Heritage Team (STScI/AURA) and J. Green (University of Colorado, Boulder). Page 16: Galilean moons © NASA/JPL. Page 17: Io © NASA/JPL/University of Arizona; ice on Europa © NASA/JPL/University of Arizona. Pages 16-17, background: Orion Nebula © NASA/JPL-Caltech/STScI. Page 18: Saturn © NASA, ESA and Erich Karkoschka (University of Arizona). Page 19: Saturn's rings © NASA/JPL/Space Science Institute; Dione © Image Credit: NASA/JPL/Space Science Institute. Pages 18-19, background: Cloudy region, Sharpless 140 © NASA/JPL-Caltech. Page 20: Uranus © NASA/JPL/STScI. Page 21: Miranda © NASA/JPL/USGS; Ariel © NASA/JPL. Pages 20-21, background: Same as pages 8-9. Page 22: Neptune © NASA/JPL. Page 23: Dark spots and Scooter © NASA/JPL; Triton and Neptune © NASA/JPL/USGS. Pages 22-23, background: M42 © NASA. Page 24: Eris and Dysnomia © CalTech. Page 25: Artist's concept of New Horizons at Pluto © Johns Hopkins University Applied Physics Laboratory/Southwest Research Institute (JHUAPL/SwRI); Artist's Concept of Kuiper Belt Object 2003 UB313 © NASA, ESA, and A. Schaller (for STScI). Pages 24-25, background: Sharpless 308 © Don Goldman. Page 26: Ida and moon © NASA/JPL. Page 27: Gaspra © NASA/JPL; Eros © NASA/JPL/JHUAPL. Pages 26-27, background: Trifid Nebula © Todd Boroson, AURA, NOAO, NSF. Page 28: Comet SWAN © Michael Jäger/Gerald Rhemann. Page 29: Comet Wild 2 © NASA/JPL; Wild 2 gas release © NASA/JPL-CalTech. Pages 28-29, background: Same as pages 16-17. Page 30: Orion Nebula © NASA,ESA, M. Robberto (Space Telescope Science Institute/ESA) and the Hubble Space Telescope Orion Treasury Project Team. Page 31: Crab Nebula © NASA, ESA, J. Hester and A. Loll (Arizona State University); Eagle Nebula © NASA, ESA, STScI, J. Hester and P. Scowen (Arizona State University). Pages 30-31, background: Same as pages 14-15. Page 32: M81 spiral galaxy © NASA, ESA, and the Hubble Heritage Team (STScI/AURA). Page 33: Sombrero galaxy © NASA and The Hubble Heritage Team (STScI/AURA). Pages 32-33, background: Hubble views NGC 4402 © NASA/ESA Page 34: Gas jets in the Carina Nebula © NASA, ESA, and the Hubble SM4 ERO Team. Page 35: Hubble against Earth's Horizon © NASA/STScI; Bug Nebula © NASA, ESA, and the Hubble SM4 ERO Team. Pages 34-35, background: Same as pages 4-5. Page 36: Cat's Eye Nebula © NASA, ESA, HEIC, and The Hubble Heritage Team (STScI/AURA). Page 37: Saturn aurora © NASA, ESA, J. Clarke (Boston University), and Z. Levay (STScI); Hubble ultra-deep field © NASA, ESA, S. Beckwith (STScI) and the HUDF Team. Pages 36-37, background: Same as pages 6-7. Page 38: Astronauts Karen Nyberg and Akihiko Hoshide © NASA/JAXA. Page 39: Astronaut Joseph R. Tanner © NASA; Buzz Aldrin on the Moon © NASA. Pages 38-39, background: Same as pages 22-23. Page 40: Space Shuttle Endeavour © NASA. Page 41: Crew on Endeavour's mid deck © NASA; Endeavour landing © NASA. Pages 40-41, background: Same as pages 24-25. Page 42: Endeavour liftoff © NASA. Page 43: Apollo 4 liftoff © NASA; rocket engine test © NASA/Marshall Space Flight Center. Pages 42-43, background: Same as pages 26-27. Page 44: International Space Station © NASA. Page 45: Astronaut Sandra Magnus © NASA; Soyuz spacecraft approaches the ISS © NASA. Pages 44-45, background: Boomerang Nebula © ESA/NASA. Page 46: Argentinean research satellite SAC-A © NASA. Page 47: Atmospheric Neutral Density Experiment 2 satellites © NASA; SuitSat © NASA. Pages 46-47, background: Same as pages 32-33. Page 48, background: Same as pages 24-25.

TP4023-1 6/10

Printed, manufactured, and assembled in Dongguang, China

10 9 8 7 6 5 4 3 2 1
ISBN: 978-0-545-24972-0
10756

Conforms to ASTM standard F963-08.

Space is the place where human explorers have traveled the farthest. Human-made machines have gone even farther, all the way out of the solar system and into the blackness beyond. And our telescopes look past that to the extreme edges of the universe, where the faint light reaching Earth has been traveling through space for billions of years. There are amazing sights in all that space, from the planets of our solar system to fiery nebulae and faraway galaxies. And now you can see them in 3-D!

Contents

THE SUN

The Sun is the star at the heart of our solar system. Like all stars, it is made of gas, mostly hydrogen and helium. The core of the Sun is a nuclear-powered furnace. There, the nuclear reaction called fusion squashes hydrogen atoms together to create helium atoms, releasing gigantic amounts of energy. The temperature at the core is about 27 million degrees Fahrenheit (15 million degrees Celsius).

If the Sun were hollow, it would be big enough to hold a million Earths.

The photosphere is the Sun's "surface," the layer we can see from Earth. (It really isn't a surface, because it's made of gas.) In this picture the hotter outer layer called the *chromosphere* (**KROME**-uh-sphere) is visible. This picture shows the Sun's invisible ultraviolet light, not the light we can see.

When a part of the Sun's magnetic field slows down, the gas rising from the inner layers to the photosphere creates sunspots. These lower, slightly cooler areas are usually twice as big across as Earth.

FAR OUT!

At the end of its life—in about five million years—the Sun will throw off its outer layer of gas and shrink to become a star called a white dwarf. The thrown-off gas will glow as it runs into particles that the star expelled before, making a huge, glowing cloud in space like the Helix Nebula.

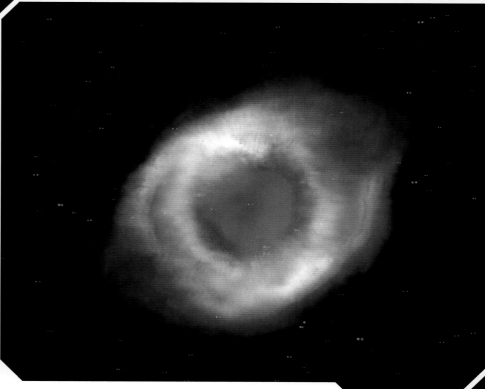

The Helix Nebula formed when a star died.

MERCURY

By day, Mercury is hotter than an oven, but Mercury's nights are colder than the deepest deep-freeze. The closest planet to the Sun is also the smallest of the true planets, only about 1½ times the size of Earth's moon. The surface temperature can rise as high as 800°F (430°C) on the sunny side of the planet.

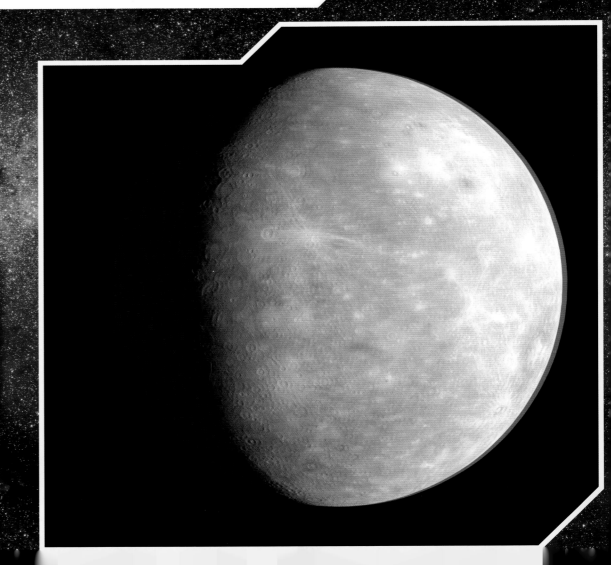

Unlike the other planets in the solar system, Mercury has no atmosphere. It has a thin layer of gas called an exosphere, made up of atoms blown off the surface by tiny meteoroid impacts and the solar wind (a stream of particles from the Sun).

FAR OUT!

Comets crashing into Mercury may have left water behind. Radar images from Earth show there may be water ice where the Sun's light and heat can't reach, at the bottom of deep craters near the planet's poles.

Mercury's surface is pocked with impact craters left by meteoroids and comets. With no atmosphere or surface water to wear them away—as on Earth—craters on Mercury remain sharp and crisp.

A scarp runs through a crater on Mercury.

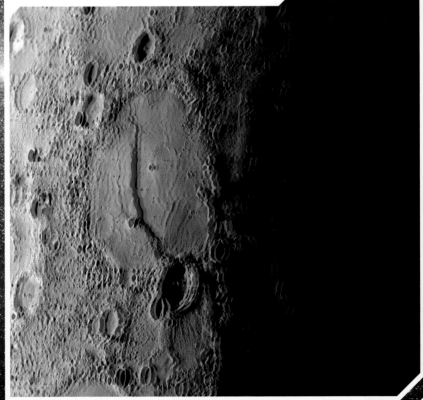

The Planet That Shrank

Billions of years ago, when Mercury was first forming, volcanoes spewed lava onto the planet's surface. As it cooled, Mercury shrank. This made the crust stronger, sealing off the volcanic vents. The shrinking crust also pushed up gigantic cliffs called scarps.

VENUS

The second planet from the Sun is almost the same size as Earth, with nearly the same gravity, but it's no place for humans. Venus's thick carbon dioxide atmosphere traps the Sun's heat like a greenhouse, pushing temperatures at the surface higher than 850°F (450°C). Venus is also the site of hurricane-force winds, lightning storms, and sulfuric acid rain.

Backward Days

The planet spins on its axis in the opposite direction from Earth, so on Venus the Sun rises in the west and sets in the east. One Venus day lasts 243 Earth days.

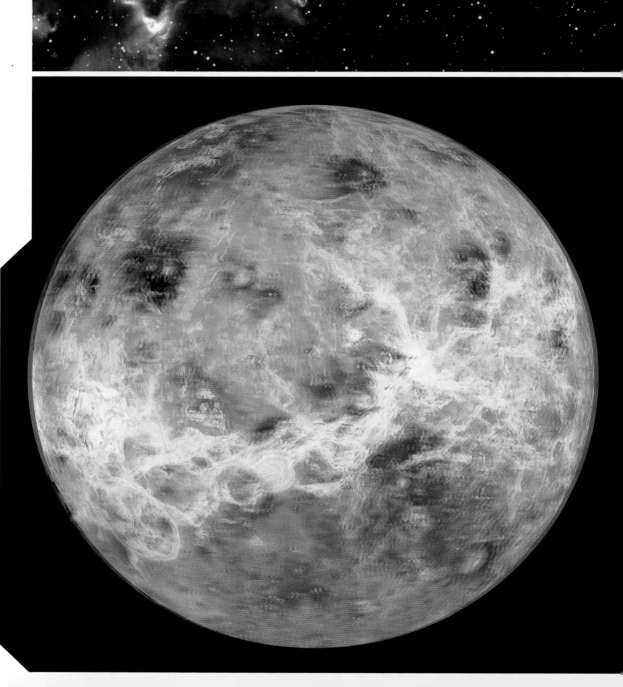

Venus's thick clouds make it impossible to look at the surface with visible-light telescopes and cameras. When the Magellan spacecraft mapped the surface of the planet in the 1990s, it used radar to capture its images.

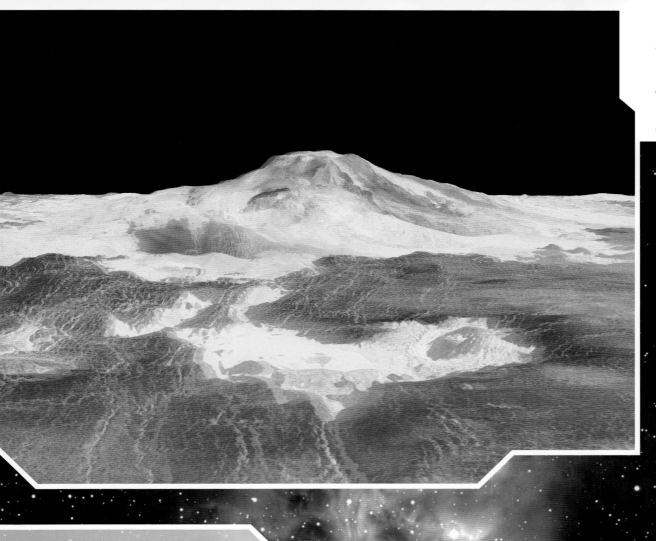

Lava flows surround Maat Mons, a five-mile-high volcano near Venus's equator. This image was created using radar information from NASA's Magellan spacecraft. The colors are based on Russian spacecraft photos of the Venusian surface. Heights are exaggerated 10 times in this picture. The actual volcano has a much gentler slope.

FAR OUT!

The temperature on Venus is so extreme, all the spacecraft that have landed there–with scientific instruments exposed to the elements–have been wrecked after only a few hours, when the delicate instruments failed.

A corona (plural: coronae) is a pattern of cracks in the surface of a planet, surrounding a craterlike depression. Scientists think these coronae were formed by magma pushing up the crust. When the crust cools and settles, it creates a sunken area surrounded by cracks. Heights are exaggerated 20 times in this image.

THE MOON

Earth's moon is the fifth-largest moon in the solar system. It's one-quarter the size of Earth, orbiting 238,900 miles (384,400 km) from our planet. The surface is covered with impact craters left by meteoroids, comets, and asteroids.

The large, dark areas of the Moon are called *maria* (MAR-ee-uh; singular: *mare*, pronounced MAR-ay). The name means "seas" in Latin. The maria are impact basins, like very large craters, that filled in with lava when the Moon was young. You can see them from Earth with your unaided eyes.

FAR OUT!

In October 2009, scientists crashed a rocket on purpose into a crater at the Moon's south pole. The crash shot a cloud of dust, vapor, and rocks high above the surface. Instruments on an orbiting spacecraft looked at the debris and detected evidence of water.

Copernicus is an impact crater, created when a meteoroid or a piece of a comet smashed into the surface of the Moon. The crater is 58 miles (93 km) across.

Earthshine, or light reflected from Earth, glimmers on the lunar surface. The glow behind the Moon comes from the Sun's upper atmosphere, visible from Earth only during a total eclipse. Venus shines in the background of the picture.

Earth's moon is the only place in the solar system outside of our own planet that has ever been visited by humans.

MARS

Earth's small red neighbor is a cold place, where the highest summer temperature is only 23°F (-5°C), and the winter low is -125°F (-87°C). The atmosphere is mostly carbon dioxide, not breathable by humans. Like Earth, Mars has ice caps at its poles, but it's "dry ice," or frozen carbon dioxide.

Mars has two moons, Phobos and Deimos.

A Martian landscape of rocks and sand spreads out to a pair of hills in this picture taken from the Mars Pathfinder spacecraft. The Martian sky gets its pinkish yellow color from dust in the atmosphere.

Water, Water Everywhere?

There's water on Mars, enough to fill Lake Michigan twice. It's mixed into the ground about three feet (1 m) below the surface near the south pole. It's frozen, of course. The temperature on Mars never gets above freezing, even on the warmest days of the Martian summer.

FAR OUT!

Mars has some extreme geology, including the biggest-known volcano in the solar system, Olympus Mons. This mountain is three times higher than Mt. Everest and covers an area the size of the state of Arizona.

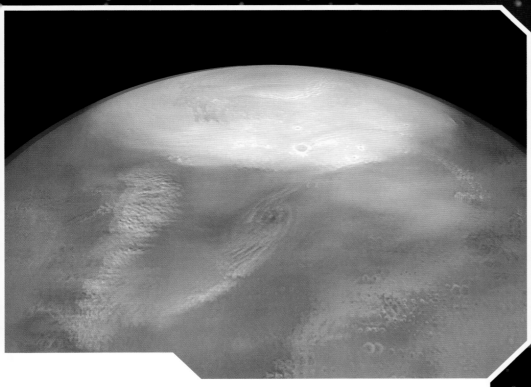

Spring on Mars brings dust storms. You can see two large patches of dust storm clouds just below the pale brown ice cap at the top of this picture.

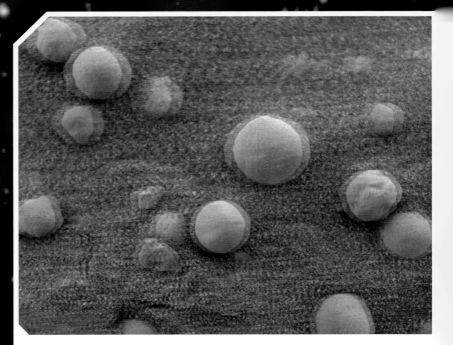

This close-up of berry-shaped rocks on the Martian sand was taken by the Mars Rover Opportunity. The actual area in the picture is only 1.2 inches (3.0 cm) across, about the size of a postage stamp.

JUPITER

The largest planet in the solar system is 11 times the diameter of Earth. It's a gas giant with no solid surface. Jupiter is made mostly of hydrogen and helium. Deep in the atmosphere, the hydrogen becomes a liquid sea, and at the very center, there may be an Earth-sized core of rock and ice.

Jupiter's clouds contain some water vapor, but they're also made of ammonia and hydrogen sulfide, a gas that smells like rotten eggs.

Clouds cover all of Jupiter with stormy patterns of stripes and swirls. The brown and white bands, called *belts* and *zones*, are created by rising and falling currents and powerful east-west winds in the upper atmosphere. The Great Red Spot, just below the equator, is a huge, swirling storm that has been observed by astronomers for more than 175 years. The spot is more than twice the diameter of Earth.

Jupiter's third-largest moon, Io (EYE-oh), seems to float above the clouds in this image from the Cassini spacecraft. But don't let the picture fool you: Io is about the size of Earth's moon, and it's nearly as far above the clouds as our own moon is from Earth.

FAR OUT!

With 62 known moons, Jupiter ties the solar system record with its neighbor, Saturn. Only 50 of Jupiter's moons have names.

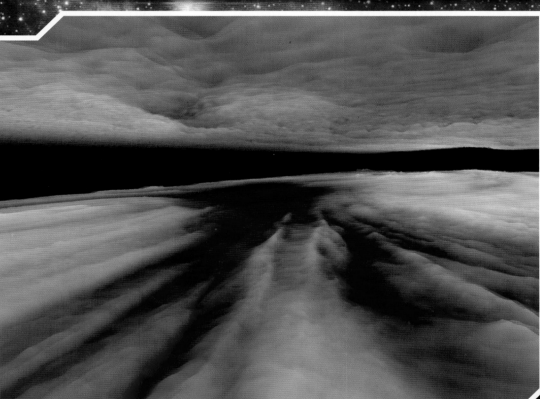

Cloud Model

This 3-D computer model shows cloud layers near Jupiter's equator. It is based on information from the Galileo space probe. In the model, the cloud layers have been simplified and colored, and the heights have been exaggerated 20 times.

GALILEO'S MOONS

Four hundred years ago, the Italian astronomer Galileo Galilei pointed his new, improved telescope at Jupiter and found four tiny "stars" near the planet. As he watched them over many nights, he realized they weren't stars at all, but moons. Galileo became the first person to discover moons around another planet.

The four largest moons of Jupiter, in order from closest to farthest from the planet (and from back to front in this picture) are **Io**, **Europa** (yer-RO-puh), **Ganymede** (GAN-ee-meed), and **Callisto** (kuh-LIS-toe). **Ganymede** is the largest, followed by **Callisto**, **Io**, and **Europa**. This imaginary scene is a combination of real images taken from the **Voyager** spacecraft.

FAR OUT!

Io's most extreme volcano, called Loki (LO-kee), spews out more heat than all of Earth's volcanoes put together.

Planet-sized Moon

Ganymede is the biggest moon in the solar system, bigger than the planet Mercury. The moon's rocky inside is covered by a very thick layer of water ice. Astronomers have also discovered traces of a very thin oxygen atmosphere on Ganymede, but it is much too thin to support life.

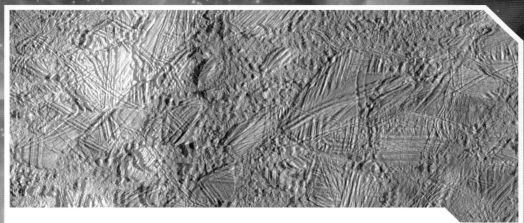

All of Europa is covered with an ocean of water. Here the frozen surface has broken into "rafts" of ice.

Io

Jupiter's third-largest moon is about the same size as Earth's moon, but there's a lot more happening on Io. It's a fiery ball of volcanoes, more than 100 of them. Huge lava flows spew onto the surface all the time, giving the moon its smooth look.

SATURN

The solar system's second-largest planet is a gas giant, made mostly of hydrogen. Far below the cloud tops, Saturn is covered with a sea of liquid hydrogen, perhaps with a core of molten rock and ice at the very center.

Saturn is the farthest planet visible from Earth without a telescope. You need a telescope to see the rings.

Saturn's orange-yellow cloud colors come from ammonia and methane gases. The large, dark gap in the rings is called the Cassini Division, named after the Italian astronomer who discovered it through his telescope more than 300 years ago.

Saturn's rings are made mostly of water ice particles, along with dust and rocks ranging in size from sand grains to truck-sized boulders. The rings are only about 100 feet (30 m) thick, razor thin compared to the ring system's 150,000-mile (240,000-km) width.

Ringed Planets

With more than 1,000 individual rings, Saturn's ring system is the biggest and most beautiful in the solar system. Uranus, Neptune, and Jupiter have rings, too.

Dione (di-OH-nee), Saturn's fourth-largest moon, seems to hover against the backdrop of the planet in this picture. The thin lines below it are the rings, seen edge-on. Saturn has 62 known moons. The largest, Titan, is the second-biggest moon in the solar system, larger than the planet Mercury but smaller than Jupiter's largest moon, Ganymede.

FAR OUT!

Saturn may be huge, but it's less dense than water. If you could find a bathtub large enough to hold it, Saturn would float.

URANUS

The seventh planet from the Sun was the first ever discovered with a telescope, more than 200 years ago. This gas giant takes 84 Earth years to orbit once around the Sun.

This image from the Hubble Space Telescope shows Uranus with its 11 rings and several moons. The bright spots near the right-hand edge of the planet are clouds. The colors in this image are modified to depict certain features more plainly: The blue areas show clearer parts of the atmosphere.

In true color, Uranus looks like a smooth, bluish-green ball.

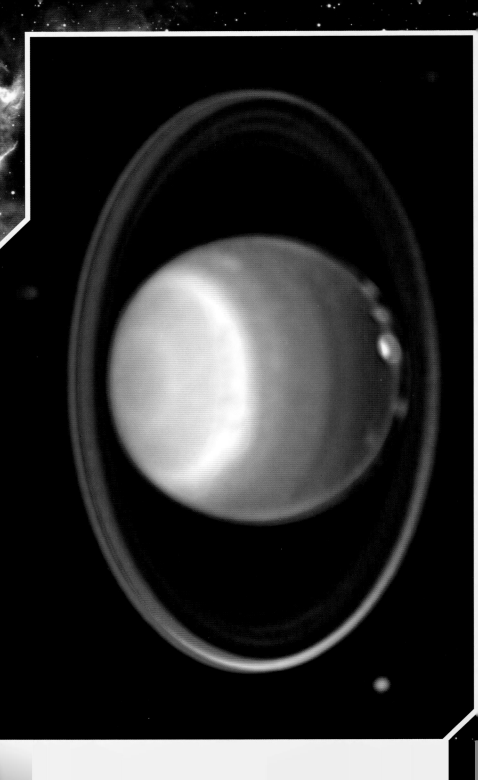

Miranda

This moon looks like a collection of parts of different moons. Miranda may have been smashed into pieces as many as five times. Gravity would then have pulled the pieces back together, with some old parts and some new ones showing.

Uranus has 27 known moons. The five largest are Titania, Oberon, Ariel, Umbriel, and Miranda. They get their names from characters in plays by William Shakespeare.

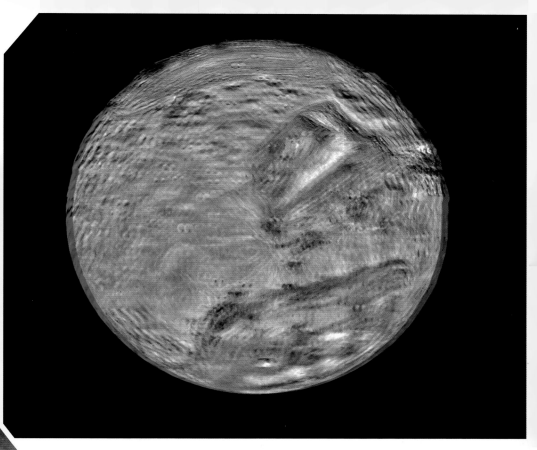

Of Uranus's five big moons, Miranda is the smallest and closest to the planet. It's only about 300 miles (480 km) across.

Ariel is the brightest of Uranus's moons. It measures about 700 miles (1,150 km) across. The surface is pitted with many small craters, but these don't show up well at the distance of this picture.

FAR OUT!

Uranus is tipped over on its side. It spir on an axis that is almost horizontal compared to the other planets that have an almost vertical axis.

NEPTUNE

The atmosphere of this gas giant is mostly hydrogen and helium, but the planet's blue color comes from methane. Neptune has 13 known moons. All the close-up pictures of Neptune were taken by the Voyager 2 spacecraft in 1989.

Voyager 2 spotted the fast-moving oval in the middle of this picture, called the **Great Dark Spot**. Later pictures from the **Hubble Space Telescope** show that the spot is gone. Scientists aren't sure exactly what the dark spot was. They suspect it was either a hole in the atmosphere or a storm.

Beneath the **Great Dark Spot** is the white cloud nicknamed **Scooter**, and below that is another dark spot. Scooter circled the whole planet in just 16 hours. Wind speeds near the equator of Neptune are more than 700 mph (1,100 kph). This is faster than the speed of sound on Earth.

FAR OUT!

Triton is the coldest world ever discovered in the solar system. The temperature there is -390°F (-230°C).

Ice Volcanoes

When Voyager 2 flew by Triton, it found geysers spewing icy liquid nitrogen and methane into the moon's thin atmosphere. The liquid freezes right away and falls back to the surface as snow.

This combined picture from **Voyager 2** shows the view you might have if you were approaching **Neptune's** largest moon, **Triton**, aboard a spacecraft. The pinkish ice cap at the south pole is frozen methane. Scientists don't know what caused the pattern resembling cantaloupe skin on the surface north of the ice cap.

DWARF PLANETS

Dwarf planets orbit the Sun and are big enough for their own gravity to pull them into a ball shape, but not big enough to clear other objects out of the area around their orbits. A dwarf planet with an orbit beyond Neptune is called a plutoid. Pluto and Eris are the biggest known plutoids.

Eris

Until 2006, Pluto was considered the ninth and last planet in the solar system. But when astronomers discovered Eris, which is bigger than Pluto, they began to debate exactly which objects in space counted as planets. In the end, Pluto lost its place as a full-fledged planet and became a dwarf planet.

This is an artist's idea of what the dwarf planet Eris and its moon, Dysnomia, might look like. The Sun is a bright dot in the distance.

This computer-enhanced image shows light and dark areas on Pluto's surface, based on information from the Hubble Space Telescope.

The New Horizons space probe was launched in 2006 on a long journey to visit Pluto and its moons. It will reach the dwarf planet in 2015. This picture shows an artist's idea of the spacecraft's arrival at Pluto.

FAR OUT!

Pluto and Eris are both Kuiper (KYE-per) Belt objects. The Kuiper Belt is a disk-shaped zone of icy objects orbiting between 2.8 and 4.6 billion miles (4.5 to 7.4 billion kilometers) from the Sun. It's the extreme frontier of the solar system.

ASTEROIDS

Asteroids are space rocks left over from the younger days of the solar system. Some of the larger objects are called minor planets. The smallest are about as long as a football field, while the largest-known asteroid, Ceres, is more than 600 miles (1,000 km) across. Most of the solar system's asteroids orbit the Sun in the Asteroid Belt, between the orbits of Mars and Jupiter.

Only one as
Vesta, is vis
from Earth
binoculars
telescope. I
the biggest
(it's actuall
third bigges
is the brigh

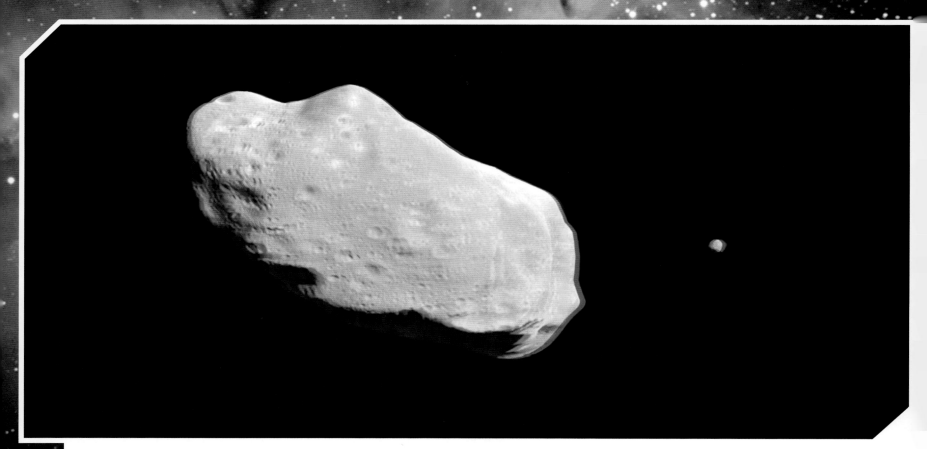

Some asteroids, like Ida shown here, have their own moons. Ida's moon was discovered when the Galileo spacecraft flew by the asteroid. Ida is about 35 miles (56 km) long. The moon, named Dactyl, is only about 1 mile (1.6 km) across.

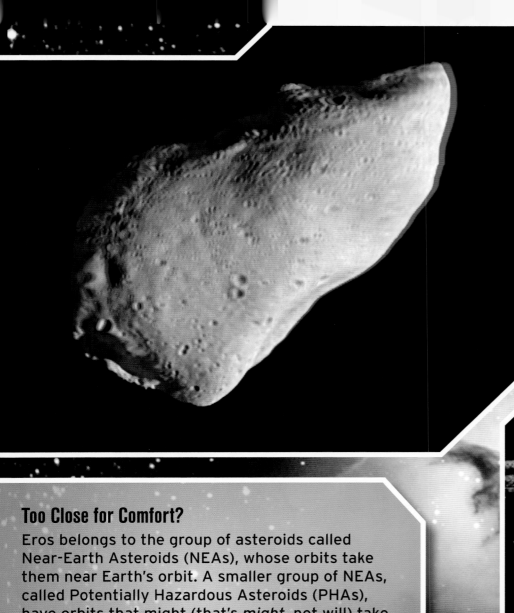

Gaspra
Crater-covered asteroid Gaspra was also photographed by the Galileo spacecraft. The part shown in this view is about 11 miles (18 km) across.

Eros
This close-up of asteroid Eros comes from the spacecraft known as **NEAR S**hoemaker. It's a combination of four images taken from about 62 miles (100 km) above the surface.

Too Close for Comfort?
Eros belongs to the group of asteroids called Near-Earth Asteroids (NEAs), whose orbits take them near Earth's orbit. A smaller group of NEAs, called Potentially Hazardous Asteroids (PHAs), have orbits that might (that's *might*, not will) take them close enough to be in danger of striking Earth. NASA keeps track of more than 1,000 known PHAs.

COMETS

Comets are "dirty snowballs" made of frozen water and carbon dioxide mixed with dust. They orbit the Sun in long, elliptical (oval-shaped) orbits, where they spend most of the time at the far edges of our solar system.

Dust and gas from the comet form a long tail, pushed by the solar wind. The tail stretches away from the Sun, but not necessarily behind the comet.

Stardust

NASA's Stardust spacecraft is the first ever to visit a comet and bring back a souvenir from the trip. In 2004, Stardust passed through the gas and particles jetting off comet Wild 2. It caught a sample of the sand-grain-sized particles in a superlight material called an aerogel. When Stardust passed by Earth in 2006, it dropped a capsule containing the aerogel into the atmosphere. The capsule parachuted to the ground and was retrieved.

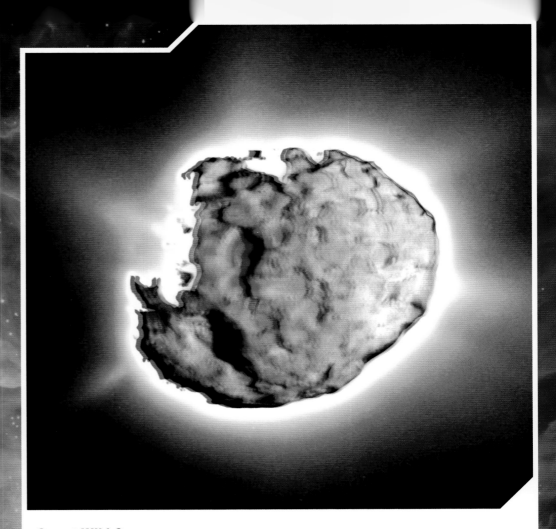

Comet Wild 2
The nucleus, or solid part of this comet, is about 3 miles (5 km) across. The comet's name, Wild, is pronounced "vilt."

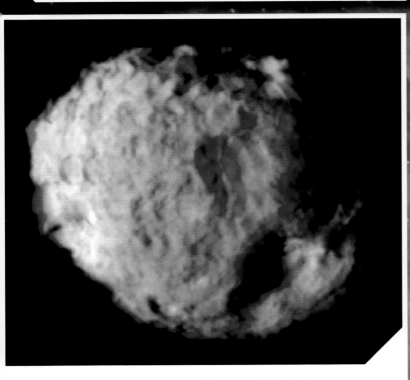

Comet Wild 2 spews out jets of gas and dust. As energy from the Sun warms the comet, frozen carbon dioxide and water *sublimate* (SUB-lim-ate), or go straight from solid to gas form.

FAR OUT!

The aerogel from the Stardust spacecraft is the lightest solid ever made. It's 99.8% air. The rest is silicon. Aerogel is light, yet solid enough to stop comet particles traveling much faster than a bullet fired from a gun without damaging them.

NEBULAE

A nebula (NEB-yuh-luh)—plural: nebulae (NEB-yuh-lee)—is a gigantic cloud of gas and dust in space. A few of them can be seen without a telescope in the night sky. In photos, nebulae show the bright, glowing colors and amazing shapes that make them some of the most beautiful sights in space.

You can see the Orion Nebula on dark nights in the winter and spring sky. Look for the constellation Orion, the hunter. The nebula is the bright star in the middle of the hunter's sword, hanging below the three stars of his belt.

Glowing gases and dust surround young stars in the Orion Nebula. Energy from the new, very hot blue stars makes the gases glow with their own light, like the gases in a neon tube.

FAR OUT!

Some nebulae—like the Crab Nebula—occur after supernova explosions. Other nebulae are formed when huge masses of gas collapse under their own weight. Some nebulae are called stellar nurseries, places where new stars are born.

Crab Nebula

At the end of their lives, giant stars (stars more than three times bigger than the Sun) explode and hurl gases out into space. The explosion is called a supernova. In the year 1054, Chinese astronomers recorded a new "guest star" that was bright enough to see during the day. The Crab Nebula's glowing gases are the traces of that supernova.

Gigantic pillars of dark hydrogen gas and dust tower against the glow of the Eagle Nebula. The biggest pillar is about 4 light-years (more than 2 trillion miles, or more than 3.7 trillion kilometers) long.

GALAXIES

Look up on a dark night, away from city lights, and you'll see the bright band of stars called the Milky Way stretching all the way across the sky. The Milky Way is our home galaxy. It's a huge, spinning spiral disk of 100 billion stars. Clouds of dark gas and dust block our view of most of them.

The spiral disk of the galaxy called Messier81 (or M81) is similar to the shape of the Milky Way. M81, also known as Bode's Galaxy, is in a group of galaxies. M81 is about 11.6 light-years away from Earth.

Where Are We?

Our solar system is about two-thirds of the way out from the center of the Milky Way, in a spiral arm called the Orion Arm. As the galaxy spins, we're moving along at a speed of 560,000 mph (900,000 kph). Even so, it takes the solar system 200 million years to make one trip around the disk.

M82

M82 is an irregular galaxy. Scientists believe that the red clouds of glowing hydrogen blasting from the center were formed when the galaxy came too close to another galaxy. M82 is about 12 million light-years away from Earth.

Sombrero

Thick bands of dark dust show in our edge-on view of the Sombrero Galaxy. The picture shows the bright bulge in the center, a feature of all spiral galaxies. The Sombrero Galaxy is about 28 million light-years away.

FAR OUT!

Scientists think the center of many galaxies is a supermassive black hole, a collapsed star with gravity so strong that not even light can escape it.

HUBBLE SPACE TELESCOPE

No matter how big their magnifying mirrors and lenses are, all telescopes on Earth have a problem they can't get around: the atmosphere. Moving layers of air bend and shift the light coming from space. The atmosphere also limits how clear a telescope's picture of space can be. This problem was finally solved in 1990, when the Hubble Space Telescope (HST) rode into orbit aboard Space Shuttle *Discovery*.

A billowing pillar of gas and dust looms in this HST image of the Carina Nebula.

Getting Glasses

After the telescope was launched, scientists got a nasty surprise. A flaw in the main mirror made the images taken by the telescope's cameras blurry. Astronauts installed a set of extra mirrors to correct Hubble's vision in 1993.

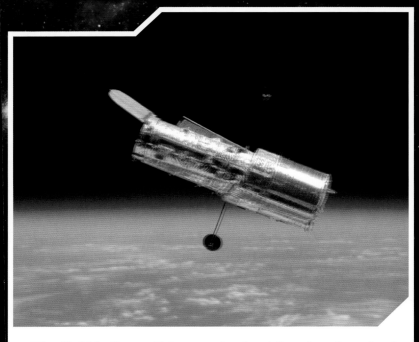

The Hubble Space Telescope is about the size of a school bus and orbits Earth at an altitude of 370 miles (595 km). It travels around the planet once every 97 minutes.

FAR OUT!

The Space Telescope's primary mirror is 7.9 feet (2.4 meters) across.

Bug Nebula

The Hubble Space Telescope took this image of the nebula NGC 6302, nicknamed the Bug Nebula, in 2009. The butterfly-like "wings" are gases thrown off by a star near the end of its life. The star is hidden behind a dark band of dust in the middle.

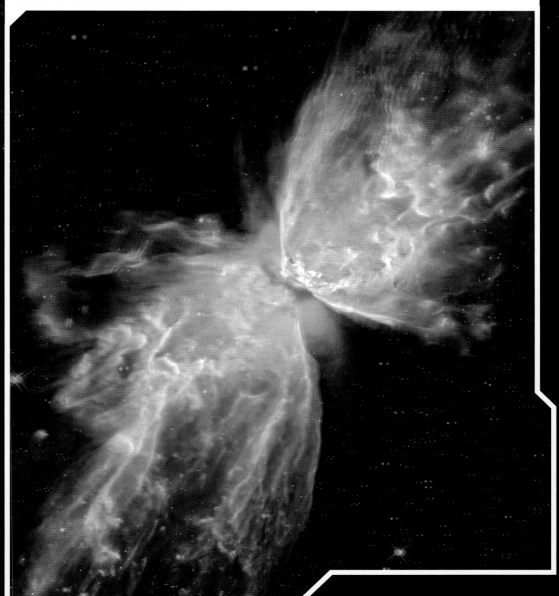

MORE HUBBLE IMAGES

The Hubble Space Telescope will keep on taking spectacular images of space until at least the year 2014, when the new Webb Space Telescope is launched. Scientists hope Hubble will still be working long after that.

The Cat's Eye Nebula, NGC 6543, is another shell of expanding gas, shrugged off by a dying star. This type of nebula is called a planetary nebula because, more than 200 years ago, these nebulae appeared in telescopes as round, greenish disks, like distant planets.

Closer to Home

The Hubble Space Telescope doesn't look only at deep space. Astronomers also use it to study objects closer to home. This image shows an aurora, like the northern lights on Earth, near the south pole of Saturn. The aurora image shows ultraviolet light, not visible to humans.

The Most Extreme Picture Ever Made

The Hubble Ultra Deep Field is the deepest look into the universe ever taken. The image covers an extremely narrow section of space billions of light-years long. Nearly 10,000 galaxies are visible in the image. The smallest, reddest ones are the farthest away.

VERY FAR OUT!

Looking into the Hubble Ultra Deep Field means looking back into time. The farthest galaxies in the image existed when the universe was only 800 million years old. (For the universe, that counts as young.) It took their light billions of years to travel through space to Earth.

ASTRONAUTS

Want the most extreme job on Earth (or *off* it)? Try being an astronaut. These space travelers go the farthest and fastest of any human being. Some are pilots, whose job is flying and landing the space shuttle. Others are mission specialists, the scientists and engineers who perform experiments and work with space technology, like the Hubble Space Telescope and the International Space Station.

Astronauts Karen Nyberg and Akihiko Hoshide work the controls of the International Space Station's robotic Canadarm2 in the Destiny laboratory.

If You Want To Be An Astronaut . . .

. . . study hard. To be a NASA astronaut, you'll need a college degree in science, math, or engineering. After that, you'll need three years of experience in your field before you can even apply for the job.

For some jobs, astronauts have to put on space suits and go outside. It's called an *extravehicular activity* (EVA), better known as a spacewalk.

EMU

The technical name for a space suit is extravehicular mobility unit, or EMU. The pressurized suit with its life support, communications, and other equipment weighs more than 250 pounds (113 kg) on Earth. In orbit it's weightless.

On July 20, 1969, astronaut Buzz Aldrin stands on the surface of the Moon, 238,900 miles (385,000 km) from home. Only 12 people have walked on the lunar surface.

FAR OUT!

The extreme speed record for human beings is 24,791 mph (40,000 kph), set in May 1969 by the Apollo 10 astronauts on their way back from the Moon.

SPACE SHUTTLE

The space shuttle is the world's first and only reusable spacecraft. It can carry a crew of up to eight astronauts and 63,000 pounds (28,600 kg) of cargo into orbit, stay there for up to 10 days, and return to Earth to be refitted and launched again. The U.S. shuttle fleet has been flying into space since 1981.

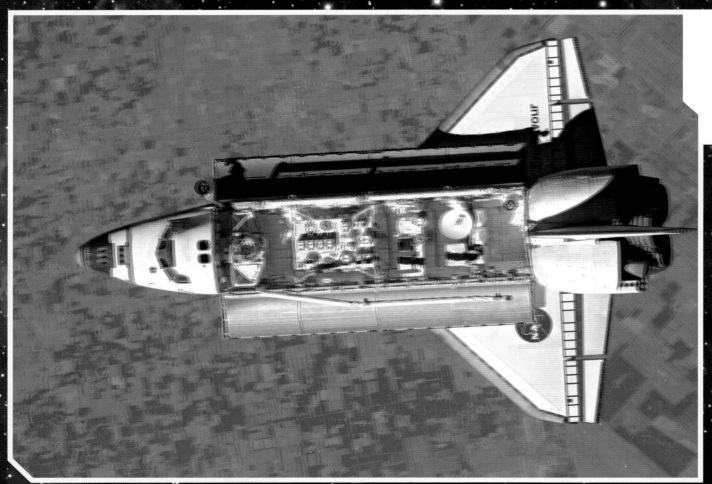

The shuttle *Endeavor*, photographed here from the International Space Station, orbits more than 200 miles (322 km) above Earth. The payload bay doors are open, showing the spacecraft's cargo area.

FAR OUT!

The space shuttle takes just 8$\frac{1}{2}$ minutes to go from 0 to 18,000 mph (29,000 kph).

Crew Cabin

The forward section of the shuttle's crew cabin is the flight deck, with the instruments and controls for flying the shuttle. It has seats for the pilots and two other crew members. Behind that is the mid-deck, with living and working space for the crew. The equipment bay and airlock are behind the mid-deck.

The shuttle isn't the most spacious vehicle inside. Astronauts have to be able to work in tight conditions.

Space Shuttle *Endeavor* lands at the Kennedy Space Center in Florida. The shuttle glides without engine power. When it lands, the spacecraft is still traveling more than 200 mph (322 kph).

ROCKETS

Rockets are the most powerful engines ever built. A rocket works by burning fuel inside its combustion chamber. The burning creates hot gases that shoot out the nozzle at the end of the rocket. The force of the gases shooting out pushes the rocket in the opposite direction.

Space Shuttle *Endeavor* lifts off, riding a pillar of flame. The clouds of steam come from a reservoir of water below the launch pad, put there to damp noise and vibrations from the powerful engine exhaust.

FAR OUT!

The large tank on the shuttle's belly holds more than 525,000 gallons (2,000,000 liters) of liquid hydrogen fuel and almost 150,000 gallons (570,000 liters) of liquid oxygen. The shuttle burns all that fuel in just 8½ minutes.

Take Your Own Oxygen

Fuel needs oxygen to burn. Rockets carry their own oxygen along with the fuel. That's how they can work in space, where there's no oxygen.

During a test, a cone-shaped rocket exhaust nozzle directs the force of the exhaust gases.

The Saturn V was the biggest and most powerful rocket ever made. It stood taller than a 35-story building and had 11 liquid-fuel rocket engines. The last Saturn V orbited Earth in 1973.

INTERNATIONAL SPACE STATION

The International Space Station (ISS) orbits Earth at an altitude of more than 250 miles (400 km). It is home to a permanent crew of five astronauts, along with temporary visitors including spacecraft crews, scientists, engineers, and even a few tourists. (The tourists paid millions of dollars for their very short visits.) The station is an orbiting scientific laboratory. The astronauts study Earth, space, and the challenges humans will face when they travel to more distant places like Mars.

Building Room by Room

The ISS is built in sections, or modules. The modules are carried into orbit by the space shuttle and attached to the station by the astronauts.

The International Space Station is Earth's permanent human outpost in space.

American astronaut Sandra Magnus reads a checklist aboard the station. The ISS has hosted crew members and visitors from 15 different countries.

FAR OUT!

The International Space Station is the largest artificial satellite (an object that orbits a planet) and the largest human spacecraft ever built. The finished station and its solar panels will take up as much area as a football field.

One Soyuz capsule is kept docked to the station at all times for use as an escape craft in emergencies.

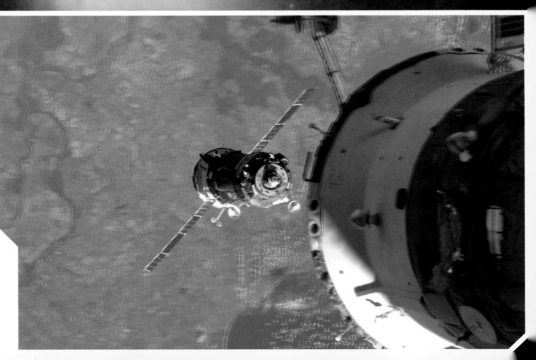

A Russian Soyuz spacecraft arrives at the International Space Station with three crew members. A crewless version of the same spacecraft serves as both a delivery ship and a garbage truck, bringing supplies to the station and taking away trash.

ARTIFICIAL SATELLITES

Until 1957, the Moon was Earth's only satellite. That was the year the Soviet Union launched a beachball-sized, artificial moon called Sputnik 1 into orbit. The Space Age was born! Today more than 3,000 artificial satellites from more than 40 countries orbit our planet.

This satellite from Argentina carries space technology experiments. It was taken into orbit by Space Shuttle *Endeavor.* One of the instruments on board is built to track whales off the coast of South America.

Satellite Jobs

Different artificial satellites have different jobs. Some point instruments at Earth to study or even to spy on the planet. Others, like the Hubble Space Telescope, point their cameras in the other direction to study space. Still others are communication satellites, relaying signals from one part of the planet to another.

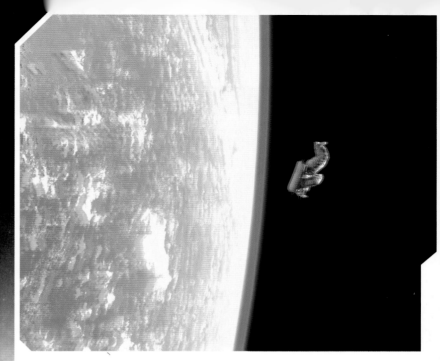

This weird satellite, called SuitSat, is a retired Russian space suit. The suit, with no one inside, was launched from the International Space Station. It carried sensors, batteries, and a radio transmitter. People around the world were invited to listen in on SuitSat's transmissions and log them on a special Web site.

A pair of microsatellites named Castor and Pollux are released from the space shuttle *Endeavor*. The satellites aren't much different in size and shape from Sputnik 1. Each of the spheres is about twice the size of a basketball. (In this photo, Castor and Pollux are the two gold-colored spheres.)

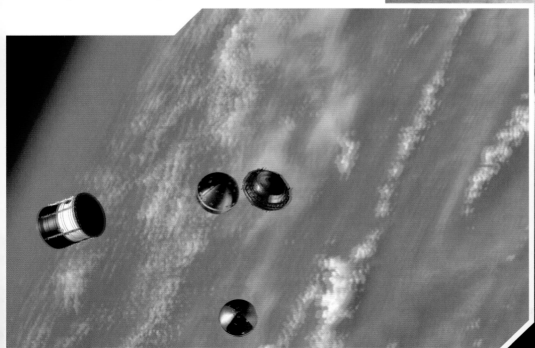

FAR OUT!

One group of satellites helps people find their way around on Earth. The Global Positioning System, or GPS, is a set of 24 satellites. A GPS receiver uses radio signals from the satellites to calculate its location on the ground.

SOLAR SYSTEM STATS

	AVERAGE DISTANCE FROM SUN	DIAMETER	DAY LENGTH	YEAR LENGTH	SURFACE GRAVITY	NUMBER OF MOONS
SUN	——	864,400 miles (13,910,000 km)	609 hours, 7 minutes (25.38 Earth days)	——	2,800% of Earth's gravity	——
MERCURY	35,983,095 miles (57,909,175 km)	3,032 miles (4,879 km)	58.65 Earth days	87.97 Earth days	38% of Earth's gravity	0
VENUS	67,237,910 miles (108,208,930 km)	7,521 miles (12,104 km)	243 Earth days	224.7 Earth days	90.5% of Earth's gravity	0
EARTH	92,955,820 miles (149,597,890 km)	7,926 miles (12,756 km)	23 hours, 56 minutes, 2.4 seconds	365.24 Earth days	——	1
MARS	141,633,260 miles (227,936,640 km)	4,222 miles (6,794 km)	24 hours, 37 minutes	1.88 Earth years	37.8% of Earth's gravity	2
JUPITER	483,682,810 miles (778,412,020 km)	88,846 miles (142,984 km)	9 hours, 55.5 minutes	11.86 Earth years	214% of Earth's gravity	62 discovered so far
SATURN	885,904,700 miles (1,426,725,400 km)	74,898 miles (120,536 km)	10 hours, 39 minutes	29.4 Earth years	106% of Earth's gravity	62 discovered so far
URANUS	1,783,939,400 miles (2,870,972,200 km)	31,764 miles (51,118 km)	17 hours, 14 minutes	84 Earth years	86% of Earth's gravity	27 discovered so far
NEPTUNE	2,795,084,800 miles (4,498,252,900 km)	30,776 miles (49,528 km)	16 hours, 7 minutes	164.79 Earth years	102% of Earth's gravity	13 discovered so far

THE STORY OF BIRTHRIGHT

AN ALTERNATIVE TO ABORTION

Louise Summerhill

Birthright International
777 Coxwell Avenue Toronto, Ontario, M4C 3C6
Phone: 416-469-4789 • Fax: 416-469-1772
www.birthright.org • info@birthright.org

Printed by Federal Graphics Inc., Mississauaga, ON, Canada
ISBN 0-913382-06-X
LCCCN 72-96117

Eleventh Printing, 2006

Photograph courtesy of Birthright® of Melbourne, Florida.

The Story of Birthright was first published in 1973.
It has been reproduced in its original form with the addition of
a preface by her daughter and current Co-President of Birthright
International, Louise R. Summerhill.

CONTENTS

PREFACE

When Birthright began in 1968 my twin sister, Stephenie, and I were on the verge of our fourth birthday. Birthright is something that we grew up with, and into, and it framed many of the events of our family and our lives.

Louise Summerhill died fifteen years ago, on August 11, 1991. With time behind us, it is compelling to look back and to understand the extraordinary person that she was. Knowing who she was, the things she struggled with, and the challenges in her life, it is no surprise that she was able to guide Birthright to the worldwide movement that it is.

A little more than sixteen years ago, when I was called to the Bar, my mother hosted a dinner of family and friends, and, in the dramatic fashion that she was so fond of, recited a poem she had written for me. It started this way:

> This all started 28 years ago
> I was quite content and happy to know
> That Billy would be starting school in the fall
> I thought I was through with diapers and all
> I thought of the time when I'd be free
> To do things for myself, to be "just me"
> To do things that I wanted, to just be quiet
> To shop for a new dress, if I wanted, to buy it.
> After all, raising five kids isn't easy
> But, I wondered, why do I feel so queasy?

The ending, of course is the realization that, after five children and at the age of 45, she found herself pregnant – and worse yet, with twins.

If THAT Louise Summerhill were here today she might re-tell the poem this way:

This all started **38** years ago
I was quite content and happy to know
That the girls would be in grade one next year
My freedom at last was so very near.
For near 30 years kids had kept me on the run
Now was the time for me to have fun.

Try as I might I could not shake the fear
That God was whispering something into my ear
The abortion issue was causing some pain
I was writing letters but nothing was gained
I thought that I should be taking a stand
But my heart kept saying just hold out your hand

And in that moment Birthright was born
and in my heart I felt so forlorn
"God, why do you ask me to carry this load?"
He said not a word, but I knew that I should.

All those years ago Louise Summerhill stepped forward, very reluctantly, in faith, and with faith. Like many Birthright volunteers, she had no intention of committing for any length of time, and she had absolutely no thought of starting an international movement. She was going to get it off the ground and move on. Move on to enjoying her children, and even by then, her grandchildren. She fought God for months on it – searched for the right leader – conceived the name and the logo. And still she defied the call. I CAN'T DO IT, she said.

One day, in June 1968, my twin sister, Stephenie, ran into the side of a car. She was lucky and not so badly hurt as it turned out, in spite of numerous stitches and consequential doctors' appointments. On leaving one of those appointments my mother, two five-year-olds in tow, stood staring at a "For Rent" sign in front of a medical building. A hand tapped her on the shoulder and asked if she was looking for an office. This was 1968. The likelihood then, that a 50-year-old woman, with five-year-old twins in her hands, would be needing an office must have seemed low. Yet there he stood, and as he heard what she was dreaming of, he asked her "do you believe in the Lord Jesus Christ?" When she said "of course", he offered her the office for free.

In that moment Louise Summerhill finally heard the voice of God – finally understood and accepted that this most unwanted child was hers to bear, and in that moment Birthright was given life. To know and understand Louise Summerhill you need to know that she cried her heart out when she realized what God was asking – she cried, I'm sure, for her lost freedom, for the lost time with her children, for the burden of being called. And in spite of those tears she stepped forward in faith to meet the scared and broken women who needed her – who needed us. In her own words in this book she describes her acceptance: "Then one day it came to me: Our Lord who had far greater responsibilities than any of us, never seemed pressured for time, to speak to the woman at the well…".

The story of the woman at the well is one that we often think of in Birthright. In the historical context it would have been unacceptable for Jesus even to speak to a Samaritan, never mind a woman, never mind one as broken as she. And yet Jesus meets her at the well – the place of community – the place of life.

And what is truly remarkable is how He treats her – with simple acceptance. The Samaritan woman is broken, but Jesus speaks to her without judgment, without condescension, with the message that she does have value – is unique – is precious. Jesus affirms the woman at the well; He loves her in all her brokenness. Just as He loves each one of us in all our brokenness.

Birthright volunteers are Jesus to the pregnant women in crisis. In the willingness to treat them with respect – the willingness to accept – the willingness to form a relationship with her, they affirm and build her confidence, her sense of self-esteem; her sense that she is worthy. When a Birthright volunteer does this, it allows her to open herself to possibilities – to see a future – to step forward in faith. Faith that someone will be there to hold her hand and pick her up when she falls. That faith is what allows her to feel hope for a future with her baby.

How did Jesus reach the brokenness of the woman at the well? What did He do? He spoke with her – He built a relationship. Jesus didn't give her things, He didn't lecture her – instead He entered into communion with her. In the words of Jean Vanier:

The heart of relationship
Is not to *do things for* people.
It is not to possess them
Or to use them for our satisfaction, to fill our emptiness.

It is to reveal to them that they are unique, precious and have beautiful gifts.

It is to live a communion of hearts with them

Where we help each other to grow to greater freedom.

Life flows from one to the other[1].

Life flows from one to the other. In communion with the women in crisis we can give life and receive life, if we recognize our own brokenness and accept our own weaknesses. If we bear witness to our past, to our own feelings of helplessness, to our own woundedness, we can receive Jesus' love and we are given new life. We can, in turn, give life.

Time and again in this book Louise Summerhill speaks of the struggles she had with what she perceived to be her own failings and weaknesses. Certainly she could have told you of feelings of brokenness derived from a childhood of pain and loneliness. As abundantly strong and determined as she was, she was raised by a father who refused to accept who she was; a father who feared and even hated her faith in the face of his avowed atheism. Not surprisingly, he coped with his own fears by breaking her down and rejecting her, almost out of hand, for her faithfulness. Many would have given in and given up. Instead she turned to that faith, and feeling the embracing presence of God in her life she chose to live, aware of her brokenness, in the affirmation that Jesus gave to her.

My mother's extraordinary ability to empathize with the women in crisis came from her heartfelt understanding of their sense of brokenness, and from her wish to affirm them with love – a love that was lacking in her own childhood. You only had to hear her on the phone, as I did as a child, with a woman in a wheelchair, under the threat of losing her child to the

---

[1] *Drawn into the Mystery of Jesus through the Gospel of John*, Novalis Publishing, 2004.

Children's Aid. Her calm, her determination, her love for that woman came through with every word, and in every silence. Louise Summerhill understood the power and the importance of presence. She knew that by "just" being, by "just" loving, she could help that woman on her journey to self-esteem and self-confidence, and her journey to love her child. She knew that love would let her step forward in faith to love and nurture the child.

Every single day in a Birthright office somewhere in the world, a scared pregnant woman, young or not so young, makes the exact same leap of faith. In spite of all her fears she hears a voice that says "You can do this." And she hears that voice above the din of the world around her. She hears it because it is the voice of God disguised as a Birthright volunteer.

That poem, by the way, that my mother wrote when I was called to the Bar, ended with her query to the doctor if there was one babe or two, and the following lines:

He said to me, get up on the table
I'll tell you right now, if I am able.
And sure enough, as you can see,
Two beautiful girls God had given to me.

At the age of 46, in spite of her anguish and her anger, my mother moved forward in faith to give birth to me and my twin sister, Stephenie. 38 years ago that same Louise Summerhill stepped forward in faith when God tapped her shoulder and said Birthright also must be born and nourished. Faith allowed Louise Summerhill to carry and nurture the unwanted baby that was Birthright and to accept and hear God's will even as she cowered with fear.

Every single day, Birthright volunteers go to their offices, and in doing so step forward in faith. They give themselves to God, and in doing that they give themselves to the women in crisis. Their faith breeds hope, and gives hope. It lifts despair and it allows the woman to see, with her own eyes, the beautiful child that God has given to her.

In the many moments of grief and despair we must remember to embrace the hope, embrace the love, embrace the faith, that Louise Summerhill had in the moment she acknowledged that God was calling her to Birthright. In the same way He has called each and every Birthright volunteer to this – for all of their foibles, for all of their fears, and for all of their faith. Together in faithfulness the Birthright community moves out into the world, through an uncertain future, but with confidence that faith will move Birthright forward in the journey, that faith will hold Birthright steadfast to its roots, that faith will move mountains of hopelessness and build futures of possibilities.

Louise R. Summerhill
Toronto, 2006

To Mary, the Mother
of Our Lord.

AUTHOR'S UPDATE

Today's generation is faced with challenges in every area of life. How we meet those challenges will determine the face of tomorrow. The future is now, and it is in our hands. Among the greatest of these challenges is the assault on innocent human life that was unleashed by the January 22, 1973, decision of the United States Supreme Court (*Roe vs. Wade*), which has had the effect of permitting abortion on demand at any time during the nine months of pregnancy.

Today we have the resources to bring the benefits of civilization to the whole world. Yet, sadly, the riches of scientific insight are all too often placed in the service of death rather than of life. Millions go to bed hungry every night, yet billions of dollars are spent in pursuit of more efficient mechanisms of death. And many millions of unborn children die without seeing the light of day.

We must recognize that it is only God who gives life. It is really God who, through the sexual union of man and woman, creates another person. "If the creative power of God be withdrawn from things," says St. Augustine, "they perish. Nor is anything... produced if God does not create it."

God has not retired. As He was in the beginning, He is now, and ever shall be, the Creator of all things. Even when conception occurs unexpectedly, outside of marriage or within it, it is God who has chosen to bring forth human life.

My personal conviction about the dignity of motherhood – without which I could not have summoned the courage to found Birthright – is based on scripture. It should, therefore, be meaningful to Protestant, Jew, and Catholic alike.

In Isaiah 49:15, we read: "Can a mother forget her infant, be without tenderness for the child of her womb? Even should she forget," says the Lord, "I will never forget you." Again in Isaiah, 66:13, we read the Lord's words: "As a mother comforts her son, so will I comfort you."

When God likens His love for us to that of a mother for her child, we can surely see the dignity of motherhood.

But the true blessedness of Mary, and of all mothers, and indeed of all of us, is to hear God's word and to keep it in our hearts. When a mother hears God's word and keeps it in her heart, she acts with the compassion that is characteristic of God Himself. In the light of God's love, becoming a mother is a beautiful and wonderful experience, one that a woman should not reject but should, rather, embrace with joy.

Children are not the possessions of their parents; still less are they the possessions of the state. All children belong to God, for it is God who created them. In Ezekiel we read: "Behold, all souls are mine. The soul of the father, as well as the soul of the son, is mine." And Jesus said, "It is not the will of your Father in heaven that a single one of these little ones should perish" (Matthew 18:14).

Clearly, as God's possessions, children have a right to be born – a *birthright*. We should keep in mind that God has a great destiny in store for every child He creates. "Let the little children come to me," says Jesus, "and do not hinder them, for of such is the kingdom of God." (Luke 18:16).

Heaven's intention for every child conceived in the womb is that that child shall achieve God's kingdom, and that he or she shall live in Christ; and, living in Christ, that the child shall pass on to life everlasting with God in heaven. All this is the child's destiny. Indeed all this is our destiny, for we are God's children too.

If we in our generation should fail to deal with the problems of our age in the way that God expects, it will be because we never achieved the vision of the world as God planned it from the beginning.

Women have always been capable of loving and giving to the point of heroic sacrifices, for sacrifice is an integral part of woman's existence. We women are the givers, the nurturers of life, and no nation can rise above the level of its women.

Sixteen years have gone by since Birthright, the very first pregnancy service, was started here in Toronto. I had no experience as an organizer, and little more than prayer to go on. From its start in a small, donated basement office, Birthright grew apace. It became a success, not only in Canada but in many parts of the world.

Birthright is vitally alive – in the United States, in South Africa, in Malaysia. Almost daily we are asked to open Birthright centres. Requests come in from Italy, Kenya, Greece, France, Ireland, the Philippines. Pregnancy services in Australia and New Zealand, though not called Birthright, got their start through our assistance, as did the first Lifeline in Great Britain.

Through the inspiration of the Holy Spirit, millions of babies have been saved by the emergency pregnancy services movement that began with Birthright in Toronto.

We have received many blessings since I wrote *The Story of Birthright* in 1972. With God's help and through the generosity of our many friends in Toronto, including private donors, the Knights of Columbus, and the Catholic Women's League, we have been able to purchase a house. At

Margarita House, a gift for which we are most grateful, we are able to provide emergency shelter for pregnant girls.

We have had our pains, our heartaches, our battles with burnout; but each time a child is saved from abortion, we are renewed. For we are cooperating in God's work, the work of creation.

Abortion statistics around the world are rising, and problems caused by our enemies multiply. Nonetheless Birthright volunteers work in peace and harmony, knowing that theirs is a labour of love. Each year, at least one and a half million unborn babies die in the United States, and some seventy thousand in Canada. But in our six hundred North American Birthright centers, and in others around the world, we are helping many, many mothers to see their pregnancies through. By this work, not only are the lives of the unborn being saved, but mothers, too, are being saved from a lifetime of guilt and remorse.

Louise Summerhill
Toronto, 1984

PRAYER OF THE UNBORN CHILD

Now, I'll never wind my baby arms around my mother's neck,

And I'll never sit upon my daddy's knee,

I'll never see the golden sun shine on my sister's hair,

These joys are meant for others, not for me.

For my life was ended far too soon within my mother's womb.

The cruel surgeon's knife made her my tomb.

My Father who created me now holds me in His Hand,

But I long to build some castles in the sand!

I'd love to pick a yellow flower,

Just once to see the sky,

It seems to me I'm much too young to die.

So Heavenly Father listen to this unborn baby's plea

Don't let mothers kill, as my poor mom killed me.

Tell them they will want us 'cause we bring our love along,

To let us live, to grow up big and strong,

My mother didn't understand because I was so small

That some day her little boy would grow to six feet tall.

Louise Summerhill

INTRODUCTION

So many letters are arriving from people enquiring about Birthright, many of these expressing a desire to establish Birthright centres in their own communities. I wish it were possible for me, personally to meet all of these people, but, regrettably, this is not so.

Until now, I have endeavored to answer all the letters and the questions contained in them, believing that, in so doing, I can help, by telling of our experiences, not only in the organization of Birthright centres, but also in spreading the word to girls who need our help. However, what seems even more important to me, is the need to impress on all, the sacredness of the mission of Birthright, and the truth we proclaim through our testimony.

I, and all those who work closely with me, are acutely aware of the Spirit of God in our midst, and we know from the miracles of grace and rebirth that we encounter daily in the lives of those who come to us, that the Creator and Sanctifier of human life is guiding and inspiring us. Again and again, He is showing us that there are practical solutions to the problems of distressed pregnant women, and that these are found in a positive and loving dedication to women in distress.

Time no longer permits me to reply in person to all the questions, so important and topical, so I have thought to offer the answers in book form. Therefore, I am retaining the style of informal conversation, as if I were talking, not to an anonymous and impersonal public, but to a group of friends gathered here at the Toronto Birthright centre.

The stories I may introduce will be true, expressing a deeply felt reality, stories of human suffering and despair, living and personal. If I seem to bring God into the picture, and quote often from the Scriptures, it is because I realize how important a part faith and prayer have in our work, and because it is my need to find daily inspiration in meditation and prayer, and from the Bible.

I ask you to be patient with me, and may God, and all forgive me if, in vanity, I take for myself, what He and many others have contributed. I have made mistakes, clear-cut errors, and I would be dishonest not to recognize these. It appears that some of these I am unable to make right. Yet, being genuinely aware of our failures, and the powerlessness and limitations of our human condition, helps us to see clearly the meaning in St. Paul's words: "Who is weak, and I am not weak, Who is made to fall and I am not indignant." (II Corinthians 11:29)

It seems to be a profound and mysterious truth that God's plan is not only accomplished by our successes but also by our failures.

It is a fact that I have not always been willing to accept my role as the founder of Birthright. It has been a constant struggle for me to bring into the world, and then nurture, this "child" that I conceived, and to which I gave birth. No mother ever delivered a more "unwanted child," nor tried harder to rid herself of what seemed an intolerable burden. It has been by the grace of God, only, that Birthright was never aborted in the embryonic stage.

For over a year I had been working with an anti-abortion group, as secretary. I was convinced that abortion is entirely destructive, but it is so easy to become deeply and emotionally involved in "lobbying" against the legalization of abortion in government, and to overlook the humane concern of our opponents for the suffering and despair of distraught pregnant women. With me, there came a gradual awakening to a general sense of my responsibility to do something positive within my own radius of action. If we remain inert in the face of evil, and find relief in making only verbal

3

protests, we seem to be much like Pontius Pilate who, in an atoning profession of faith, inscribed on the cross "Jesus of Nazareth, the King of the Jews." (John 19:19) The more I understood about the abortion problem, the greater my burden, the heavier the weight of my own responsibility.

Perhaps some of you have heard of a group called "Abortion Anonymous" who, in Birmingham, England, operated a telephone service offering to arrange abortions secretly for girls and women, distressed by unwanted pregnancies. This was before the law was liberalized.

I could see this only as destructive, and tantamount to the suicide centre offering help to kill oneself, and Alcoholic Anonymous helping one to become intoxicated. Gradually a plan began to take shape of a similar type of telephone service, exclusively for pregnant girls and women, but offering, instead, counsel and positive aid to carry their babies to term, that is, alternatives to abortion.

After thinking it over for several weeks I spoke to a friend and spiritual advisor. He liked the idea and encouraged me to develop it. "If one life is saved," he said, "and just one girl helped from abortion, all will be worthwhile." Yet I doubted, reluctant, and afraid of failure. It was this priest's gentle and calm persuasion which gave me, again and again, the strength I needed to go on.

There were also doctors: my own, Dr. Gerald Solmes, and also, Dr. Patrick Beirne, whose enthusiasm spurred me on; and many other clergymen, Fathers John Kelly, C.S.B., Frank Skumavc and John Moss, who gave hours of their time to working on the problems of organizing. Rev. Dr. Graham Scott, a United Church minister, was also a tremendous help and inspiration. Then there were women, some personal friends, whose help was invaluable, and to all of these I owe a debt of gratitude.

Nevertheless, the task loomed far too great and if, with clear conscience, I could have given the task to someone else, I would gladly have done so. Yet, inwardly, I knew that this was something God was asking of me, personally, and I could not seek excuse by hiding behind my husband and children.

"I have no time," the inner dialogue went on, "My duty lies elsewhere." I knew that I would leave myself open for severe criticism for neglecting my children if I took the job, and I also knew that this might almost seem justified at times. Five of my seven children were still at home, the youngest being six-year-old twins, and the job of raising them, of cooking, washing and cleaning was enough to fill any woman's day.

Then one day it came to me: "Our Lord, who had far greater responsibilities than any of us, never seemed pressured for time, to speak to the woman at the well" (John 6: 1-26), "to admire the lilies of the field" (Matthew 6: 28), "or a sunset" (Matthew 15: 2). Most of all he had time to go into the desert and pray. And it was in prayer that I found the answer, then, as I do so often today.

Every once in a while I have to discover the decisive importance of prayer in my life, such as, when I find myself missing morning mass and meditation to do a basket of laundry, missing the time God is asking me to listen to Him before listening to the world. The laundry will always, somehow, get done, but I am not able to re-live those lost moments with God when I have been led by worldly consideration, no matter how worthy, rather than by personal inspiration.

It is at times of prayer that we re-discover ourselves, and find the inward peace that the world so much needs. How can we bring to other people what we, ourselves, do not possess? How can we help others to organize their lives if our own are in turmoil? In prayer we discover the correct order of values, a clear distinction about what is really important, and what is secondary, or possibly, even dangerous.

It was through prayer that I finally came to the decision to go on with Birthright. Summer of 1968 had come, and although much groundwork had been done, it was still not too late to abandon the project. As yet, no large donations had been given, and I knew that I had not gone past the "point of no return." I was so discouraged by setbacks and the loss of a close friendship, that I could not see my way clear to take up, in the fall, where I had left off.

My friend and spiritual adviser, again, encouraged me, impressing me with the importance of the work. With God's help I came to the decision to carry the "child" I had conceived to term. Thanks be to God, Birthright was not aborted. On October 15th, 1968, Birthright was born.

1. THE ESSENCE

The essence of the Birthright service is love. We should not underestimate the power of love. We do not need professional training in order to listen, to understand, to love. The fact is that the caseworker who is guided by knowledge more than by love, will experience only failure in her human relationship. True compassion recognizes no boundaries nor lays down any conditions.

Recently, this was brought home to us, very clearly, by a lovely young pregnant girl, unmarried. She had come from a distant province, and we helped her to find accommodation and placed her under the care of one of our doctors. As we do with all the girls, we directed her to the right agency for adoption procedure. This gentle and sensitive girl, intelligent and well-bred, told us that the only times she felt guilt-ridden to the point of suicide, were after she came from the appointments with her social-worker. Thank God these cases are rare, but they do happen.

Although many of my co-workers are nurses, and some teachers, many with post-graduate degrees, none of us have training in social work. I regret this of course, because I do not undervalue the importance of this type of professional training. However, when needed, we have access to the community services, and the social workers connected with them, and we have no hesitation about calling them. We, in Birthright, rely on intuition, common sense, and a loving receptive attitude, free from all judgment.

Judgment vanishes with love. We do not meddle in morality, and knowing this, girls come to us without fear of being made to feel more guilty than they already do. And who, amongst us, can say they are guilty? We are all alike, forgiven sinners.

Because we do not know them, the girls give us their confidence, and we in turn, listen without prejudice. Then, as they unburden themselves of their deep distress and feelings of guilt, they become healed by our virtue of non-judgment. Every time we experience this we are overwhelmed and see it, once again, as a sign of God's grace: "God is love and he who abides in love abides in God" (St. John's Letter 4: 12).

When we have discovered a living truth we find it most difficult to put into words, and I am afraid of shifting the accent from the realm of the heart to the realm of the mind.

Love means to care and serve and be responsible for other people, so that, as soon as we see another in distress, we immediately respond. It involves us in a loving service, and demands from us concentrated effort and dedication. It requires that we increase our skill and knowledge in order to serve others better, to have a genuine concern and love of people.

All of us are frail and inadequate and sinful and only in discovering these things about ourselves, can we truly grow up. We have to do more than listen, tolerate and understand. We have to go further even, than giving our strength, our shoulder to cry on. We must be able to say "Your pain, your weakness, your sins, are mine."

How I wish I could convey to you the great value of love and non-judgment in this work, but I know, that it will only be when you experience this miracle yourselves that you will fully understand it.

A few months ago a girl telephoned me at the office. She had just discovered that she was pregnant, and like so many others, she could think only in terms of abortion as the answer to her problem. It was true that her pregnancy had come at a most awkward time, and she saw herself dismissed from her teaching position, scorned by friends and family. No amount of persuasion could convince her otherwise, and the more I tried, the more abusive she became. I explained adoption procedure, and she cried. "I love my child too much to give it away," and severely I reproached her, "Do not speak to me of loving your child when now all you want to do is to kill it." She started to weep and as the tears flowed, repentance came, and we were able to discuss the future. The defenses down, she even spoke happily of the child. We established a bond of love which has never been broken. Nevertheless she weakened again and decided to go through with the abortion. I did not speak to her, but the message she sent me was brutal and frank, and it hurt, "Tell Louise, to hell with Birthright. I am flying to England to have an abortion." My only recourse now was in prayer. I knew I had said everything that could be said, and now it was up to God.

Time went by and we did not hear from her until recently. She asked to speak to me and again the tears flowed in embarrassment, as she asked me to forgive her. She told me her story, that just as she was stepping on the plane, she changed her mind and now she was asking, humbly, for our help to see the pregnancy through. Once again love had brought about its transforming miracle. There was no doubt about her liberation and re-birth.

In rare cases only, as with this girl, some can be helped if their mistakes are pointed out and if judgment of them is formulated, provided it is done with a helpful, non-critical approach. Severity is sometimes the measure of love. Like surgery, it may be the only way to heal. yet, even as I say this, I cannot but denounce the crushing effect of judgment. Some people die under the surgeon's knife. Girls must be welcomed with no sign of criticism, as persons of worth and dignity. Criticism blocks the way to grace and our voice drowns out the voice of God which can only be heard in silence. If girls seeking abortions are to recognize their wrong-doing, it will be in the quiet of recollection, or in the kind atmosphere of a talk with someone who will not criticize, but will love.

Let us take counsel from the story of Job who was innocent and yet struck down by misfortune and illness. His friends claimed to be speaking for God, and wished to drive Job to the confession of some sin by which he might have drawn down his sufferings upon himself. Job was revolted and the fervour with which he defended himself hardened him in an attitude of recrimination against God. It was necessary for Job's friends to be silent for Job to hear God and be reconciled with Him.

God's judgment is always quite different from ours. That is the reason Our Lord said "Judge not." Let us notice that He did not say "Judge not wrongly." We are to be free of all judgment. Judgment is destructive.

I, myself, wilt under judgment, and am so vulnerable that I am liable to be paralyzed for days by the destructive elements of judgment. I lived through just such an experience two months after opening Birthright, when three women whom I trusted, not approving my methods of directing, approached several of the doctors and clergy with a long list of accusations. Even though I was able to vindicate myself, with the help of God, reaction set in, and I was in a state of collapse for the entire day afterwards. For weeks I felt too paralyzed almost, to continue the work and it was then I realized the value of my co-workers who carried much of the responsibility for me. A retreat, at which the tears flowed copiously, finally freed me.

You could say that it was my ego and that I am hypersensitive and you could be right. Nevertheless this experience has given me a keen awareness of the dreadful effects of judgment of the innocent and the guilty, and who can say, other than God, which is which.

Only love can bring about the true understanding necessary in spiritual communion with another person. Information is intellectual, but communion is spiritual, and although we need information to achieve communion, it is only through communion that we understand people, not as cases, but as persons. When we have established a communion of love with a person, only then are we, each, able to show ourselves, as we are, without acting a part.

The supreme and universal need of all of us is to find God. Sometimes people say to me "I wish I had your faith."

There have been times, I regret to say, when my faith has become weak. When it should have been at its strongest, or so it seemed to me, when Birthright had just come into existence, I found my faith at its lowest ebb. This happened not long after opening office, in early November, 1968, and I was tormented by doubts. Beset by seemingly insolvable organizational problems, and difficulties in my home, exhausted from lack of sleep, I found myself in tears, frustrated and ready to abandon Birthright and God. It was my husband who came to my rescue with his sound common sense, by sending me to a lawyer who was able to see the solution. He advised the selection of a board of Directors to help carry the burden. In this way I weathered the storm.

Although for Birthright and myself it turned out for the best, yet it showed me how inadequate my faith was in time of adversity. My greatest failing here was, that, under the guise of charity, I was too unassertive and would assert myself only when backed against the wall. I needed the Board of Directors to give me support. Also again, the tremendous loyalty of some clergy and friends, was a great consolation to me. I owe a debt of gratitude here, and my heart and spirit are bound to the lesson I learned from their loyalty.

Yes, I too have my times of non-believing. If God has chosen me as His instrument in the founding of Birthright, it must be because of my weakness, and dependence on Him and others. By a strange inversion of values, God appears to so choose those who do His work, and we see this all through the Bible – in Jeremiah, who would have liked to hide and remain silent "My heart is breaking wildly," he says (Jeremiah 4: 20) and even in David, scorned and persecuted by King Saul – forgotten even by his father Jesse (1 Samuel 16: 6-12). Nevertheless in my case, perhaps this gives me a keener sensitivity and understanding of girls who come to me, making it easy for me to love them immediately, and be identified with them.

When a girl is oppressed by the pain of betrayal by the father of her child, it is difficult not to become emotionally involved, and more especially so if we have experienced betrayal by a friend we deeply love, and still love. I had such a painful experience in the year of founding Birthright, during its months of gestation. Each time I hear the story of betrayal pour from the heart of a sobbing girl, I feel once again, in my innermost being, the deep pain of my friend's betrayal and desertion. When a girl whispers of her love and pain, I also am oppressed, and her pain, indeed, becomes my pain. We need first-hand experience to produce in us this personal responsibility to another person's suffering.

The truth is that the girl who sobs out her disappointments, her failures, her faults, may be nearer to the Kingdom of God than I who listen to her, and I come nearer to God, and to her, as desperate as she is insofar as I recognize that I am as guilty, as powerless, as solitary. Only then can I truly love her and help her, for then I am one with her, in my repentance and my need for God.

True love is seeded in pain and since love and pain are inseparable companions, we in Birthright, where the essence is love, are experiencing deeply the wounds of this love. Now, at times, I receive letters and phone calls of distress from Birthright directors, asking for guidance and prayers. There are stories of bitter struggles for power with volunteers, of misunderstandings with board members, when they cannot see Birthright in true perspective. The need of so many North Americans is to be so statistical, and record-keeping looms larger than helping girls. Yes, love is bringing aching hearts and sleepless nights to many Birthright directors. To these I say, trust in God and live one day at a time.

2.　THE IMAGE

It took me several days to decide whether or not to write this chapter. I knew it to be important and yet I thought that having previously stressed so often the importance of the loving, non-judgmental approach of Birthright it would not be necessary to speak of the importance of creating the right image. It seemed to me that if we are sincere in our endeavour to give a compassionate, loving service, that we could not help but project the right image.

Then I thought of Alan Fujiwara whose business and profession is "image building" and who designed and donated the Birthright symbol. Alan's sound advice did much to help give Birthright the right public image, not only by designing the symbol, but by impressing on me, from time to time, the need to keep all advertising on a dignified plane. This advice has "paid off" because certainly Birthright is well accepted and highly respected in this community.

We have tried to keep the internal structure of Birthright as informally organized as possible and I will admit that this has caused much criticism amongst a few women, used to committees, who could not see this method as being successful. Nevertheless, I believe this to be important, especially in the beginning, because it allows greater freedom of action on the part of everyone, including the executive director.

I hope to deal with this in detail in another chapter and I mention it here because I believe that it is this image of approachability and informality, of non-structure, non-establishment, which has attracted and held so many volunteers, or so they tell me. In a way we imitate the type of informal structure used by Jesus during His three years of ministry.

However, we can well imagine that had He been born in the 20th century He would have made good use of modern techniques of advertising, and the communication media, and so should we, as long as we avoid any hint of being a bureaucratic, highly organized agency. If this should ever happen to Birthright, our effectiveness will begin to wane. After all, if pregnant girls need help there are already agencies giving it, but many girls shy away from agencies.

True fact is that Our Lord did make full use of images again and again in His ministry. In the Parable of the Prodigal Son, the picture of the father's arms outstretched in forgiveness, has brought liberating peace to millions because it makes us realize that the love and forgiveness of God has no conditions. Even before the son made a confession of guilt, the father's arms were already opened in welcome. In using this picture, Jesus knew the vital need that all of us have, of finding someone absolute, someone unfailing, through all life's sufferings, wherein every trust is limited, every hope is disappointed, every friendship and human love has its conditions, and where we can count on this someone to love us unconditionally.

Alan gave me quite a lot of sound information on image-building and I have his permission to pass it on to you. First I will tell you how I met Alan. It was in March 1968, and I had been speaking to Father Frank Stone, C.S.P. about Birthright. Father Stone is Director of Catholic Communications and he was keenly interested in our work and the abortion problem. He said to me, "How about calling a friend of mine, Alan Fujiwara, and telling him you were talking to me and that I suggested that he design a symbol for you."

So that was my introduction to Alan and through him, also his brother, Dr. Fujiwara. Also, that is how we got the symbol of which I am tremendously proud. The "B" with the telephone handset resembling a fetus, is now well-known from coast to coast. Someone aptly nicknamed it "the pregnant B."

Now I will quote what Alan has to say about the importance of the right image. "What is an image – what is this word that is very much – and very loosely used in many contexts?"

"The ramifications of establishing and supporting a corporate image can be as intricate as your most complicated computing machine, but in actual fact, the presenting of an image is an inescapable reality. All things that you see, touch, taste, hear or smell provide you with images of themselves. You smell a particular odour – it immediately conveys to your mind the image of a flower, or a sizzling steak, or a peeled onion. The slamming of a car door can convey to you the image of the car itself or of the driver climbing out of the car."

"This is one sense in which the term 'image' is used – the most literal sense. But it has, in modern parlance, a more significant connotation; –"

Some of you may project the image of a dynamic, lively character, full of ideas and energy, or the image of a self-contained, retiring individual. You may be a person of artistic and creative ability, inspiring others with theories and ideals, or you may be the practical down-to-earth type who knows what he wants and sets about getting it. So you are type-cast. You are regarded as the "quiet type" or the "conservative type," the "aggressive type" or the "martyr type," the "self-assured" or the "fearful type." And according to the image you project you will attract or alienate others. And it is the consistency of the image you present that begins to clarify and identify an individual as a person, so we must see the necessity for a consistent presentation of the image of a group to clarify and identify the whole association. The process of clarification and identification is the "building process of the image." For this reason, all Birthright, operating under our Service Mark, must be consistent and uniform in every area. This is one of the reasons all Birthright centres must follow the official Charter Document if they are to legally use the name.

Alan again:

"For acceptance or success in any field, it is essential to present a good image. The science and art of imagery must be developed to appeal to that section of the population that is to be influenced. Industrial and commercial corporations are very much aware of this fact and are willing to spend millions of dollars on developing and maintaining their desired images. Where the image is weak or unfavourable, the business will suffer."

Now when I first met Alan we had not settled on a name for our organization and he and I discussed the importance of just the right name, one which would not be 'gimmicky.' So, not long afterwards, I was mulling over all the possible names, dismissing one after another as they came to mind, when I suddenly said, "What has every pregnant woman? – the right to give birth – and every child? – the right to be born." Birthright! Of course! That was the name we must use! I called Alan on the phone and he also thought it suitable and went ahead then and designed the symbol.

Now back to images! Birthright, being an entirely new type of service should be careful not to be identified as a "lobbying group," working for further changes in abortion legislation. I honestly think that this would weaken the influence with the girls we hope to help, and would alienate many in the community.

Now as I said before, I did work with the organization for the "Defense of Unborn Children" but as soon as I decided to organize

17

Birthright I resigned. I felt that we should present, from the beginning, an image which may be favourably accepted by the entire community. Also, I needed all my energies for Birthright.

I think, also, that it would be a mistake to be known as denomination. Now, I am a Roman Catholic, and of course, most of my contacts are Catholics, so much of the help, financial and otherwise has come from Catholic priests and laity. Nevertheless, I am strongly in favour of becoming ecumenical or inter-denominational and I try not to over-emphasize my own religious affiliation. The fact is that, as time goes on, many others of different persuasions who find abortion unacceptable, have approached us offering help, including many Jewish people.

In the beginning I contacted the various large denominations in the community. Most were favourable to our work, and the Presbyterian Church of Canada has, officially, morally backed us, although not financially. The Anglican Church was receptive also, and I was invited to talk to Bishop Hunt, the suffrogon bishop of Toronto, and spent a pleasant two hours with him. My contact with the Baptist Church was also successful, and now, three years later, the Lutherans are freely coming forward in almost ardent support. Although these churches, with the exception of the Presbyterian Church, did not give actual official support, for the present at least, I believe that all were favourably impressed, and my making contact with them, before opening, helped greatly in projecting the right image.

We also contacted and met with representatives from the various community services. This seemed necessary, not only for practical reasons, but to let them understand what we hoped to accomplish, and that we were not trying to interfere with their work, or duplicate it. Also we knew that we would have need again and again of the community resources and this has proven to be true. Now we find we are recognized by the agencies, and many social workers are now asking for our co-operation in helping with the girls. Also, some maternity homes have requested lists of our Ontario Birthright offices.

Now in our discussions, Alan also insisted on the need of a road map as guidelines in planning the right image, and the following are some I believe suitable for Birthright.

1)   An analysis of the problem
2)   An analysis of the area of society we wish to help
3)   An analysis of our policy regarding procedure
4)   An analysis of our aims and objectives

The following four chapters will deal with these.

However, before going on, I do wish to point out that Birthright, now more than ever, must follow closely the basic principles I laid down here in the founding office. Birthright is a registered Service Mark in Canada and the United States and we must be assured that all chapters offer the same non-sectarian, non-moralistic, non-judgmental alternative to abortion. We must insist that Birthright offers person-to-person contact, and not be just a referral agency. Also, we do not become involved in contraception or sterilization, because it is not our function, being simply an emergency pregnancy service.

If Birthright chapters are deviating from all or any of these principles, no matter how much good they are doing, they are not operating in the true Birthright spirit, and therefore, are expected to change, to upgrade their service, or, in honour, to use another name. Birthright's image must be uniform from coast to coast.

All true chartered Birthright chapters must be protected, for their own sake, but most of all for the thousands of girls who seek out our help. The name "Birthright" in every city, from coast to coast, all over North America, to every pregnant girl who needs us, must have the same essence and follow, as closely as possible, the vision of its Founder, the creator of human life. More will be said later, on the vast problems facing us in some areas, from people of good will who, unfortunately, cannot see the true image of Birthright.

3.   THE PROBLEM

There is no frontier to suffering and in Birthright we reply to the whole suffering person by treating each "de facto" situation. "You give them something to eat," Jesus said to the Apostles (Matthew 14: 16). All pregnant girls need, of course, medical care, but most of them need more than this, far more than only technical advice.

A young girl of twenty who had had an abortion talked to me on the phone. She told me of her experience, and that if Birthright had been in operation at the time it would never have happened to her. She sobbed quietly as she talked: "I gave up. I went to a doctor, not because I wanted to be told I was pregnant: I already knew this. I went because I wanted to talk to someone about it and to find out if I could get some help, somewhere. When he told me, I started to cry and he seemed uncomfortable. I got the idea he was busy. I wanted to tell him that I'd like to have the baby if only I knew where to go, or what to do. Instead I left. I felt so alone and discouraged and deserted that I went and had an abortion. What else could I do?"

Most doctors understand the need of integrative medicine and that, at times a patient may need more than just technical help. Is any human question purely technical? There are times when it is important for the whole organism, for the psychological and even the spiritual life to be given a treatment.

Recently, I heard of a gynecologist who believed that when he gave medical advice he had done his duty, leaving the rest to the psychologist and the clergy. One day a girl came to his office to find out whether or not she was pregnant, and after confirming that she was, he dismissed her. Pregnant or not? For this girl his technical answers had immense repercussions because it affected her whole life and her hopes of marriage. She went home and committed suicide.

It is here I would like to denounce the false shame still widespread today, which presents sexuality in its entirety as culpable, a false shame which so many people believe to be biblical in origin. In reality the Bible speaks of sexuality with simplicity and realism. The fact is that it is in the sexual field that social suggestion causes the greatest ravages, awakening the most distressing and tenacious guilt. It is in this area that other people's judgment shows at its most destructive level. However false the social suggestion may be, it generates a real sense of guilt in the unmarried pregnant girl, which can poison her life for years to come and against which she will have a long and dramatic struggle. If she has an abortion, the sense of guilt is then ineradicable and crushing.

One girl offered to help in Birthright by telling other girls of her own tragic experience with abortion. We let her do this occasionally because it helped them, and her. She said that she had been engaged to be married and the wedding was to take place in a year's time. When she found out she was pregnant she felt too ashamed to advance the wedding date. The boy supplied the money and she obtained an abortion.

The abortionist came to her apartment and no traces were left of his having been there. The next day the girl started to hemorrhage, was rushed to the hospital and lay close to death for two weeks. Now the doctor tells her that she may never have a child. The wedding has now taken place but at 23 she faces, possibly, a childless future. She has told me that she lies awake in the night, weeping, arms aching to hold the baby she never allowed to be born. She now realizes that social judgment would have been a small price to pay for the life of her baby.

So, in spite of the more realistic attitude today to the unwed mother and child, we must admit that still, within and without the churches, moralism is wide-spread. Our struggle then is against a moralistic denegation of it. The Church proclaims the grace of God but moralism creeps in.

I once heard a zealous Christian say that she would do nothing to help these girls because they "deserved what was coming to them." This is not an uncommon viewpoint. Recently, a worker left our employ because she could not condone our attitude of total acceptance of sinners.

We have been so proud of our technical, cultural and economic achievements that we have thought in some instances that we have no further need of God, and now we find our world is crumbling. There are social and political upheavals all over the world, revolt and revenge by the outcasts of society.

The fact is that today there is a crisis of values which creates a paradoxical situation. Young people who comprise our future adult society, often live a life with material comforts never before known to man, but on the other hand, with a dearth of meaning, of direction, of clear and definite purpose.

This crisis of values which exists today and is not always recognized because we are a part of it, makes it difficult to see the family and children in their proper perspective, that is, as the centre of the scheme of things. Therefore, in spite of the marvelous advances in education and community help for people in trouble, they still fall short in fulfilling the greatest need, genuine love and compassion. Some individual social workers and teachers do place value on these things and put hours of interest into them, but society, in general, is for the most part, concerned with other things.

In every city there is a great increase in the number of illegal abortions as the problem of unwed motherhood has reached an all-time high, and if abortion is legalized the rate will go even higher. Most women who have abortions, do so because for various reasons, they do not wish to assume the role of motherhood at this time. The girls who come to us are, for the most part, unmarried. Quite a few are divorced, but the majority are girls who, believing themselves in love, discover, after pregnancy occurs, that the love affair is not encompassing enough to include a child or motherhood. These girls do not choose abortion for its own sake, any more than any other woman but rather, as an alternative to social ostracism or forced marriage. The unmarried girl who becomes pregnant must face emotional and social problems not apparent to the married woman.

It is difficult for a single girl, especially a young teenager to obtain confirmation of pregnancy. She is very hesitant about seeking medical attention, being afraid that the doctor may contact her family. She is embarrassed, of course, and hesitates, because of this, or of lack of funds, from having a 'lab' test.

At first we were fortunate in having the offer of free tests done at a laboratory, which was a great help to the girls and to us. However, we found as the need became greater, that we must become more efficient, and finally investigated the possibility of doing our own tests. In our area, this is possible by law, and a technician from a well-known laboratory came to our office and demonstrated the method to the volunteers. The cost of materials is reasonable and it is an excellent way of meeting a distraught girl and helping her over the shock of finding herself pregnant. If she is not pregnant, it is a good opportunity to show her that we must be responsible for our sexual acts, realizing that another human being can be brought into existence by the beautiful and mysterious sexual power we have. By the way, I wish to point out that we, by no means rely completely on these tests, and, if the girl is willing, we follow all tests with a doctor's appointment.

(The tests, according to the information from the company which sells them, are, if directions are followed, quite accurate. They should be done about two weeks after the first missed period. This is, evidently, sooner than confirmation through internal examination by a doctor, which is usually possible only after the second missed period.)

ACCEPTANCE OR DENIAL OF PREGNANCY

If the pregnancy has been confirmed, the girl is faced with the dilemma of either admitting she is pregnant, and making the necessary adjustments in her life, or of seeking some means to avoid going through with the pregnancy.

Some girls threaten suicide. According to some psychiatrists, however, this danger is remote. It seems to be a proven fact that the suicide rate of pregnant women is much lower than that of non-pregnant women, especially if single. The reason given for this is, that it is so instinctive in a woman's nature to protect the child, that she, rarely, will take her own life if she is with child.

Recently, we received a long distance call from a girl who said she would be arriving in Toronto the next morning and wanted us to arrange an abortion for her. She said that she could accept nothing but abortion as the solution to her problem and if she could not abort she would kill herself.

Since she was extremely distraught, we said we could meet her and at least discuss the matter with her.

I contacted one of our gynecologists who thought it best to have a psychiatrist see her as soon as possible. However, the first psychiatrist, a woman, and the one he recommended, suggested that we simply take her to the emergency entrance of a hospital. There was a total lack of any sensitivity for the girl and her problem. Naturally, we did not follow her advice which was totally contrary to the personal, loving approach of Birthright. All attempts to get an appointment with another psychiatrist failed, and the best we could do was to obtain an early morning appointment with another of our gynecologists, a very understanding woman.

I talked with the girl as soon as she arrived, and managed to reassure her of all help possible, without mentioning abortion. That evening, one of our volunteers, met her at the office, and the girl sobbed in Peggy's arms for two hours. With the tears went all the desire for either abortion or suicide. The next morning she saw our doctor and calmly decided to have the child. Once again love had performed the miracle about which a psychiatrist had been unconcerned. Perhaps this girl might never have carried out her threat of suicide but, at least, we did not take a chance and I think the story teaches a lesson to those who think only professionals belong in our work. It, really, takes both the professionals and the trained volunteers to operate a truly successful Birthright centre and all need genuine concern. Like the Good Samaritan, we must be "there" with love and compassion for "on the spot" help.

Now living in this abortion climate, many girls do immediately consider abortion. On all sides we hear how a woman has the right over her own body or that the fetus is only a piece of tissue, and part of her body, and that the awful crime is to bring an unwanted child into the world.

A woman does have the right over her own body, but the unborn child is, in no real way, a part of her body. He has his own heart and other organs, his own circulating system and blood supply. His tissues are different from the mother's, in every cell, and his blood may be incompatible. Most of all he can be of opposite sex, and how can male sex organs be part of a woman's body? The truth is, the fetus is someone else's body.

When a girl calls Birthright she is reminded, gently, of these facts, if she seems set on abortion, and when she comes to our office, she may be shown pictures of the different stages of development of her baby, and, often this brings home to her that this is a little human being who has a right to live. (We do not show pictures of aborted babies).

A few girls, especially if they are very young, consider running away from home when they find they are pregnant. Of course this does not solve the problem of pregnancy, because they simply take their problems with them, even adding to them. Most girls dread telling their parents, more for fear of hurting them than anything else. However, our experience in Birthright is that most parents, after the first shock is over, will "rally round" and give help and support to their daughters. The fact is, we have parents call us, many times, for guidance in helping their daughters. This is a time a girl really needs her mother and, if she runs away from home, she is running away from the one person who truly loves her and who will help her.

Nevertheless, there are varying types of help, and we must realize that there are mothers who "help" by arranging abortions for their daughters. If these mothers realized what this can do for their daughters' love and respect for them, if they had to listen, as I have, to the heart-breaking sobs of girls who, psychologically have been damaged for life, I believe they might realize that the best help they can give their daughters is all the love and moral support needed to carry the child to term. If they can do this, they will, some day, find out that they have become very close to their daughters, and have earned a very cherished place in their hearts. Do mothers realize that, in arranging, or persuading their daughters to destroy their unborn children, they are destroying, not only their own grandchildren but also the opportunities to demonstrate the depth and reality of their own love. Many times I have heard a girl say, "My mother only cares about herself and what people will say." So, sometimes, actually today, girls want to get away to save the lives of their babies. May God forgive these mothers!

We read, and hear, so much about unwanted children. Unwanted pregnancy is very common, but few babies are really unwanted. Dismay at eight weeks can become joy and anticipation at eight months, and, if honest, gynecologists must admit to the truth of this statement. As for the single girl who places her child for adoption, with hundreds of childless homes now waiting for babies, how could anyone speak of unwanted children?

A word here also for childless couples wishing to adopt. Could you find it in your heart to open your homes, and your lives to children of another race or colour? I believe this is something we must face, if we are honest in our needs and desires and readiness to love. Do you have the courage to learn to love any baby, to love as Christ loves? And what about babies with physical defects. These children need love more than any others.

INVOLVEMENT OF THE FAMILY

For a very young girl, that is, under sixteen, it is important that the parents be involved. Doctors do not, as a rule, give medical care to a very young girl without parental consent. If it is a case of statutory rape, the parents may wish to take legal action although most will not do so, especially if the father of the child is quite young. Also, this could have a devastating effect psychologically on a girl.

In Birthright we meet with the girl and, generally, persuade her to see a social worker from the Children's Aid. We believe these situations require professional counselling. Nevertheless, I had one experience of distraught parents of a fifteen-year-old who had been most dissatisfied with the advice given by the social-worker. I directed them to one of the maternity homes where the girl could continue her studies. In Birthright, when parents are involved, we simply show them the possible solutions and allow them to choose. A few guidelines pointed out to the parents, leaving the choice to them, seems best, as proven by the many grateful parents who have called to thank us.

With older girls, I think it may not always be the wise move to involve the family unless her decision to keep the child is clear. These girls will seek abortions, mainly out of fear of social ostracism if family and friends find out about their pregnancies. If a girl is old enough, she should be given the freedom to decide and we, in Birthright, must help her to keep her secret. Given this help, to leave town, or hide in some way, throughout the pregnancy, she will often then freely choose to have the child. The chain of Birthright centres which is forming from coast to coast, will facilitate the assistance given to many girls who wish to live out their pregnancy and confinement away from their towns. Recently, I was able to send a girl from Toronto to Calgary, and we, in turn, have helped many girls from both the Eastern and Western provinces, and Northern Ontario.

WHETHER OR NOT TO MARRY

With regard to *teenagers*, it is as a general rule most unwise for them to marry because the girl is pregnant. Marriages of this type are rarely successful, and for their sake and the child's, other solutions should be sought. Again, however, professional counselling should be found for such a couple as many factors are involved, especially the state of maturity of the young people. Care should be taken not to oppose the union too strongly, and here the advice of the clergy can be helpful. Most ministers, priests and rabbis are experienced with this problem, and can make wise judgments about whether or not a couple should marry. We must always remember that Birthright's service is basically assistance not advice.

With the older girls, in most cases, we have found them more reluctant than the boys to marry because of the pregnancy. However, there are also cases where the boy wishes to terminate the relationship as soon as he learns the girl is pregnant. This is a critical period for the girls and they suffer greatly here. I think I shall never forget the pain in the dark eyes of a very beautiful girl, who, without a tear, told me it was for this reason she wanted to be sent as far away as possible. We chose Scotland because I have contacts there. When she told the man who had taken away her virginity that she was going to have his child, he simply said "How do I know it's mine?" and walked out.

Nevertheless, these are not common occurrences, and most boys suffer also, in their own way, and do all they can to help. As a rule it is the girl who hesitates to marry as she does not want it thought that she "forced" the boy to marry her. We have had several weddings taking place after the child is born, one, not long ago, after the birth of twins. In this case, it was a particularly happy ending for the girl. She had planned, from the beginning, to keep the child, and when the twins arrived it shattered her hopes for a time. There was no way that she could see it possible for her to raise two babies single-handed. The boy asked her, again, to marry him and she did, which solved the problem.

THE QUESTION OF ADOPTION OR KEEPING THE CHILD

If a girl is in her teens, she must keep in mind the problems of her education, her means of income, the effect on the child and her chances of marriage. If the girl is older, keeping the child may be the answer, but each case must be evaluated individually, and of course, with professional help.

Generally speaking, if a girl keeps her child she loves him, and love is the most important ingredient in child-bearing. Nevertheless, she must also be able to support him, with perhaps some subsidizing, and here, I believe, is where our welfare system should be changed. I know I have been criticized for helping girls to have babies who may have to be supported by welfare. Nevertheless, our greatest asset, and our hope for the future of our country, is in our people, and not in technology as some would have us believe. Many countries today, Japan being one, and Russia another, have come to realize this, after long and bitter experience in destroying future citizens by abortion. Japan is now a country of old people, facing a serious labour shortage, and Russia, I understand, is giving medals to women with five children and more.

Many people have been "brainwashed" by the myth of a population explosion, even in the face of a steadily declining birth rate in the North American continent. In an article which appeared in the Kansas City Times, Thomas S. Jermann PhD. warns us of the danger of listening to irresponsible scare tactics which may divert public attention from the real problems of society which then go unresolved. Dr. Colin Clark, the noted British economist, also 'debunks' the myth by pointing out the need of people for a good economy. History has proven again and again that this is true. Therefore, we should be happy to invest in the welfare of our future citizens by giving help to mothers.

Many are afraid that if a girl has her baby, rather than an abortion, that she will become pregnant readily again. We have found this, by experience, to be untrue. We have had very few repeated pregnancies. If a girl is helped by love and therapy, to see why she became pregnant out of wedlock, if she is encouraged to a sense of responsibility for her sexuality, if she goes through the long heartbreaking months of pregnancy and the pangs of birth, she will have grown a great deal emotionally, and otherwise. On the other hand, abortion treats symptoms, not causes, and if we give a girl an abortion this year, she may very well seek one again next year, and the next. One wonders if young men would wish to marry these girls with a history of repeated abortions, a complete denial of motherhood and womanhood.

It is relatively easy to get an abortion and it can become even easier. Therefore, in Birthright we make ourselves easily accessible by telephone, to listen, to guide the girl or woman, not only to the best medical care, but to a discussion of her social, economic and emotional problems, and the solution to those, other than abortion.

Most of the married women who seek help do not want the child because of financial or marital problems. Contrary to what one would expect, most have only one or two children. Not long ago one young woman phoned, asking for an abortion because although she had only two children, and money was not a problem, her husband wanted her to get rid of the child because her pregnancy would interfere with their snowmobile weekends.

Some are just depressed at the thought of enduring another pregnancy, and even Christians can be thoughtless in their treatment of the expectant mother. A few weeks ago I witnessed an incident in my own church on Sunday morning. A young pregnant woman, holding a very active two-year-old climbed over another woman, and, in spite of this woman's disapproving looks, sat in the pew beside her. The little boy immediately began to make whispered "tooting" sounds as he ran his tiny truck on the seat. I sat behind him, and although distracted in my prayers, I was intrigued by his delightfully normal actions. I always feel these little ones are so close to the Lord's heart, and so precious. However, obviously the woman beside him did not share my views. As Mass progressed she became obviously stonier and irritated, and finally deliberately rose from her seat and moved several seats away. The young expectant mother, with tears in her eyes, got the message, picked up the little son and departed from the church. These, and other distasteful incidents, imprinted in her memory, will make the next pregnancy most unwanted and unbearable to face. I think every mother can remember with dreadful clarity, similar incidents during her pregnancies.

I recall clearly, three weeks before the birth of my twins, being told by a "friend" that we should be "ashamed" to bring two babies into the world.

What damage can be done by the uncharitable word! Always remember, that a great number of abortions are being performed on married women. We may, by an unguarded word or look, have a share in the killing of their babies.

4. PEOPLE HELPED

During the six months before opening office, I wondered so many times if our project would be a success, that is, if the pregnant girls would come to us. Sometimes I would lie awake at night, thinking how momentous the task was, and feeling weighed down with my own inadequacy to cope with such a responsibility. There were many dark hours when I begged God to relieve me of the responsibility, and to choose someone else, yet paradoxically, I felt compelled, by some inner drive, to continue. Against my will, a strong protectiveness concerning Birthright held me from allowing it to be harmed by good people who might guide it in the wrong direction. And it was phenomenal how many of these there were, who could not see the vision as I saw it, and these included friends, and to my greatest sorrow I lost some of these. Today, four years later, many good people still do not see Birthright as it truly must be.

Even now, as I write this, at a time when I am doing all I can to put Birthright into capable hands which will help to guide centres in the U.S.A., my heart is heavy. Our friends across the border, and some in Canada, are so highly technical, and hyper-efficient, and are perhaps, at times, prone to sacrifice sensitivity for efficiency. They cannot seem to see that the uniqueness of Birthright, that the secret of our success, is its informality and approachability and non-structure. Some fail to understand that we are not dealing with things, but with human beings. I beg of any Birthright person reading this now, please do not get "hung up" on formalism, professionalism and super-efficiency, which will mean only the "kiss of death" for Birthright.

I have never worked in the business world, nor held office in any organization. I was married quite young and there were babies around for so many years. For twenty years I had studied theology, and was familiar with the writings of some of the great theologians, and although all this might have been conducive to contemplation, it did not exactly prepare me for business. However, I could never see Birthright being run in a formal business-like manner. I had never conducted a meeting, nor attended too many to see how this was done, and to committee women, this was a dreadful outrage, and they let it be known to me. But others loved it, and came to me to tell me so. I wanted everyone to feel they could come close. I knew also that formality would drive many away, and Birthright would die before it lived. Jesus drew the people to Him by His informality and approachability, and His love, of course. This should be the way Birthright operates, – not disorganized – Jesus chose twelve Apostles – but informally, organized. In this way only, will it truly succeed, be truly a mission of love and grace.

Of course, I had tremendous support from many people, and without their help, I could never have gone on. Nevertheless there were those who believed that the agencies were adequately handling the situation, and our service was not needed. That we were needed, I never doubted. The thousands of abortions in Toronto a year cried out to heaven for something to be done, something or someone to reach out to these girls with love, and understanding and compassion, instead of judgment.

September 1968 came, and with it my decision to continue. Things became hectic with the training program and other problems too numerous to mention here. I prefer to deal with them in another chapter. One evening, a month before opening, the phone rang, just as I was preparing dinner. It was Larry Wilson, a newscaster of CHUM radio. The conversation went like this:

"Are you Mrs. Summerhill of Birthright?"

"Yes I am. Can I help you?"

"This is Larry Wilson of CHUM and I have just been speaking to a young girl of 21. She called us to find out if we could help her to locate you. She is alone, broke and four months pregnant. Tomorrow morning an appointment has been made with an abortionist by her boyfriend. She is terrified. Can you help her?"

Immediately, I thought of how unprepared we still were, but, could we say "No"? I took her name from Larry (Denise, we shall call her) and her phone number. A medical appointment with one of our doctors was made for the next day, accommodation was found, temporarily, and within a few days Denise's whole life, and outlook, had changed. Not only that, we knew now, that we were not only needed, desperately, but that the girls would come to us. It was the inspiration we all needed and I have always believed that God sent Denise to us, not only to save little James but to encourage us to go on.

Five months later Denise delivered a nine-pound boy whom she decided to keep. The following is a letter I received from her:

"Dear Mrs. Summerhill and Staff:

I would like to thank you from the bottom of my heart for the happiness which you helped bring to me. Life means so very much more, now that I have James.

However, without your assistance and Mrs. Crawford, I would never have been able to come through the difficulties.

I appreciated your kind and deepest thoughts and words of consultation. If, at any time, you wish to visit please do not hesitate. My heart and door are always open to such wonderful people. I will never forget you all.

All the best in the future.

Denise."

Today, Denise will soon be married to a young doctor. This is just one of dozens of stories of heartbreak changed into joy because of Birthright. Not long ago Denise came to the office with her little boy and I said to her, "Denise, just think, he almost wasn't," and she replied "I just shudder to think he almost wasn't."

Some of the girls who phone are quite young, around fifteen or sixteen, but the majority are in their late teens and early twenties. This is the age, it seems, when a girl finds it most difficult because, usually, she is more or less on her own. When they are quite young, they will as a rule, tell a counsellor at school, or their parents. Most often, they get the help within their home. If they phone us first, and many do, we urge them to speak to their parents or to a close relative or family friend, such as a doctor or clergyman. Very few of them have need of further help from Birthright although the parents very often then call us for guidance.

Some of the girls are college students either living at home, or in residence. There are, surprisingly, quite a few nurses, due, no doubt, to the fact that these girls are well aware of the grave dangers of abortions, and seek other help, if available. We had teachers come to us and their problems are more difficult to solve, because of their teaching contracts. One girl was a lawyer, another had her M.A. in sociology, another was a youth counsellor.

Recently, we helped a 39-year-old social worker, pregnant herself, and ashamed of her condition.

The fact is, however, that most are nice average girls. Many come from good family backgrounds, and when we look at these lovely vulnerable young mothers-to-be, it is not difficult to love them all and go "all out" for them. In every large city, there are hundreds daily crying out for mercy, for help, whether they seek it or not. When we see them we know we must do all in our power to keep them out of the hands of the abortionists, who care only for the money, and nothing really for the mother herself, and the child who must die to fill their pockets. We ask again and again "How can doctors do this despicable thing, that is, daily, dealing in death?"

More often than one would believe, the boyfriend will call to find out if we can procure an abortion for his girl. We have found that, in most of these cases, he is very impressed to learn how dangerous abortion is and will then do what he can to dissuade the girl. If the boy is shown that the girl needs him to support her throughout, he soon finds that she is grateful to him for this. One girl brought her pregnant friend to the office and we were able to do what she could not accomplish, save her friend from the abortionist who was to see her the next morning.

Many girls, we know, have been saved from possible suicide, and another, according to her mother, had gone into a state of such depression that even psychiatry did not help. Yet, a Birthright volunteer, an obstetrical nurse, was able, by telephone alone, to speak to her, listening for hours until the girl "came out of it" and went on to deliver. Believe it or not, we still do not know her real name, nor for that matter, the names of many we help.

About ten percent are married women. I wish it were more, because it is said that the greatest number of abortions are performed on married women. Those who come to us are extremely distressed, as a rule. Sometimes just talking it over is all they seem to need. Others need financial and marriage counselling. One young mother was greatly helped when we obtained for her, through the St. Vincent de Paul Society, clothing for all her children, and a layette and furniture donated by the Catholic Women's League. We also guided her to free dental care for her children.

Not long ago, one married woman had become pregnant by her husband's relative. This was a tragic situation since the affair was known in the family. Psychiatric help was made immediately available and arrangements will be made to place the child for adoption.

There are cases of divorced and separated women, pregnant by men other than their husbands; or widows even, and when there are children involved, the problems loom large and almost insoluble. It is difficult for children to understand their parent's sexuality and needs.

On college campuses and in big-city apartments there is a marked increase in the number of young couples living together without being married, many doing so openly. When this results in pregnancy, abortion is often the solution they seek. Many then regret it and find that it terminates the relationship. The reason is, of course, that the girl never really forgives herself, or society, for permitting her to destroy her own child. If the father of the child allows or encourages it, something in the relationship dies along with the unborn child. Perhaps it is something in the mother herself which dies and a lifetime of psychiatry, even of sincere repentance, cannot bring it to life again. What kind of society do we now have which speaks of liberating women, but dooms them to an imprisonment of guilt?

One young man called us about just that kind of situation. He was still living with the girl but she had had an abortion and refused to be intimate with him again. He was very disturbed because he was in love with her and hoped to marry her. However, from what he told me, there seemed little hope of a meaningful relationship being ever established again. Had he supported her to have his child, it would have been a different story. Men need to realize this fact.

The truth is that thousands of girls and women have already been given some kind of help in the first four years of Birthright. This is not including the hundreds more who place calls to our office after hours. The telephone is answered by a tape-recording with information. Encouragement is also given, along with the time of the office hours. The following is our present tape message.

"Hello, this is Birthright, an emergency pregnancy service. If you are distressed by an unplanned pregnancy, whether you are married or single, no matter what your circumstances, we will do our best to help you, free of charge, and with complete secrecy.

Please do not consider having an abortion, either here in Toronto, or most especially in New York State, where many abortionists care only for their own financial gain, and nothing for the girls whose bodies they mutilate. Even under the best of conditions, abortion is dangerous, and it is claimed by some doctors to be the most risky operation in gynecology. The truth is that if you have an abortion and survive the dangers of blood poisoning, embolism or excessive bleeding, you could be sterilized and the child you now carry would then be your only one. Records show that one third of teenage girls aborted are never able to get pregnant again.

Do you realize that your baby's heart was beating three weeks after conception and that he is a human being who someday may thank you for the gift of life? In Birthright we believe in the right of your child to live, the birth right.

So, have courage, have this baby. Even if you are unmarried, you are a person of worth and dignity and even more so when bringing new life into the world. Why not let Birthright share the burden of your pregnancy with you? The essence of our service is love.

Now, do you need a place to stay, in Toronto, or elsewhere, or do you need employment, or medical care – or, a free pregnancy test – or do you just need someone with whom you can talk over your problems and yet remain anonymous?

Our office is staffed... etc."

Frankly, if I lie awake now, it is not to wonder if the girls will come, but rather to wonder if we will be able to cope with the demands placed on us. Not only are we saving lives, we are entering into life as it is lived, the reality of life. In Birthright, we believe that we cannot stand on the side of the street and watch a huge and forsaken crowd pass along. We must get into the roadway and mingle with that crowd. Ours is not an ecclesiastical priesthood, but it is nevertheless, a solemn and sacred mission, because when girls come to us, and bare their souls, they ask for, not only our technical help, our sympathy, our solicitude, our encouragement, and our love, but also, perhaps, at times, the divine grace, which alone can efface guilt.

Now the following is a letter from an unknown woman which I have been asked to publish. I hope she will read this book and see that I have done as she asked.

May she know, in reading this, that all that she has suffered, will, now perhaps be a means of saving other women from the same tragic fate, and that, in this way, her unborn babies did not die in vain.

Dear Mrs. Summerhill:

If a woman asks you for an abortion, please say "NO." 30 years ago I got pregnant, and I told my husband that I wouldn't have the child. I went to a druggist and he gave me something and I aborted the baby. Not only that, I did it again two years after. May God have mercy on me. I murdered my own flesh and blood.

I know now that I could have managed. You always do. I have five beautiful children, all grown up and I've tried to be a good mother to them. I could have gotten along with the two others, but I killed them.

So tell all who want abortions not to do it, or like me, they'll live in misery for the rest of their lives, knowing that they deliberately killed their own.

A Mother

P.S. Please publish my letter if you can.

5.   OUR POLICY AND PROCEDURE

In a Birthright centre it is very important to develop a good working system. In saying this, perhaps I will seem to be contradicting myself, because I have stressed so often the dangers of being too structured. Nevertheless, although I believe it to be true that over-organizing can hinder, rather than help, the smooth and free operation of Birthright, there must be some systematic procedure.

Here I would like to explain why I am against formalism and conformity in Birthright. We tried it for a time, and it did not work, and I think it is because formalism stifles, not just people, but the inspiration of the Holy Spirit. In reality I like to think of Birthright in terms of a community, a group of people sharing a common purpose, striving to live more deeply the life of the Spirit. Our work is a means of expressing, realistically, our need to live our faith at a deeper level, by responding freely and *individually* to the needs of our neighbour. Each of us brings our own special gifts to share with, not only the girls who come to us, but, also with each other.

The fact is that I know I could not survive under formalism, and many people feel the same way. There may be a place for it in other organizations, but not in this one. During the early months of planning, I made appointments, met people, went hither and yon, whenever the Spirit moved me: talking, getting people interested, and enlisting the help of doctors, clergy or lay people. I was happy because I was free and progress was made in leaps and bounds.

Then I made my first major error. I chose a committee of women I admired, because they were competent in women's organizations to which they belonged. For a time it worked well, but just as we were getting established, I found myself no longer free; imprisoned, stifled and unproductive. Being a free spirit, I finally rebelled when I saw that I was expected to have an appointment with a lawyer or an accountant.

Already I have mentioned the effect of this on me, personally, when I almost abandoned Birthright and God. It was my husband who saved me, and the organization, by his sound business sense. "You have put almost a year of your life, and ours also, plus a good sum of money into this and you're not going to quit now. Dissolve this committee and go to a lawyer right away."

I followed his advice. There was a young lawyer working for a large corporation firm here and he had offered his services, without charge. So I went to see him and his advice was to incorporate as soon as possible and to choose a board of directors. I sent out letters to this "committee", explaining the new "set-up" and, thanking them of course, I asked them to continue as telephone volunteers. They chose otherwise, and there were some unpleasant repercussions, by mail and telephone, to doctors, clergy and even to my spiritual adviser and the Income Tax Department. All gave me an opportunity to explain my position, with one exception, a priest who refused to speak with me again. This was a devastating never-to-be-forgotten experience.

I realize that I find it difficult to speak of this episode, that I know I cannot discuss it objectively and altogether rationally and that perhaps I should omit telling about it. However, the letters of enquiry which I have received have made several requests concerning the "pitfalls," and so I feel a responsibility to bring this out, because to be evasive here would not be particularly helpful. Today I am glad. In some Birthright chapters, amazingly, this story has been repeated, and the suffering persons have found consolation in knowing I went through this also.

Although I see here very clearly my own faults and limitations, I believe that through this episode wherein I almost lost my way, we were able to re-discover our bearings, and work out a very good system of operations. Since then, several volunteers have confided to me that, had we continued with the committee, they would not have stayed with us. I know this is a fact because many are "turned off" from joining women's organizations because of the committees and thus, unavoidable cliques.

When I met with opposition, the natural question for me to ask was "whose fault is it? Mine or the other person's?" Perhaps it was neither. Perhaps it was just that I did not see completely God's plan and that even resistance can be in the will of God. I have always been impatient by nature. Above all, let me not fall into a spirit of judgment. Also St. Paul, in speaking of the resistance to the preaching of Jesus, said "Their trespass means riches for the world." (Romans 11: 12). Birthright had to suffer the pangs of birth and it was not easy.

I think we know that the Light which shows up our faults is the Light which heals, and this is our human condition that we must experience setbacks and disillusionment in order to discover the breadth of God's grace. "I came, not to call the righteous, but sinners," Jesus said (Matthew 9: 13).

In all of this, we lost five volunteers and the support of one priest. We still had over seventy-five, all enthusiastic and co-operative. We got together in order to work out a system of operation. Without any formal structure, we now have women holding positions which they fill, effectively, with intelligence and initiative. Unburdened by formalism, these women are free to bring forth their own talents and creativity, and I also, as at the beginning, am at liberty to plan and work and write as the Spirit moves me. The fact is that, seldom has so much been accomplished for so many by so few and all in the Spirit of love. "The love of God surpasses all knowledge," and here is the secret in the success of Birthright. We are, indeed, a community of love.

THE SYSTEM

i.   TELEPHONE VOLUNTEERS

One of the main jobs is that of telephone volunteer coordinator and one of the volunteers has worked out a very good system here. I never interfere with her method and I know the women like her and want to cooperate with her.

She keeps the list of telephone volunteers and each have been assigned a shift of either two hours in the daytime or three hours in the evening. Our office hours are from 9:30 a.m. to 4:30 p.m. and 6 to 9 p.m. from Monday to Friday. There are two telephones requiring two volunteers. Four volunteers for daytime shift of two hours each, and two volunteers for evening shifts, requiring 30 volunteers per week. This also requires a substitute staff, most especially in the winter with illness and transportation problems. Most of the volunteers are women, but, during the two summer months, we have had three seminarians to answer the phones as an experiment, taking shifts along with a woman. Now we know that men can also be used on the phones and that girls will talk to them. Occasionally, a girl will ask to speak to a woman and for this reason we keep a woman also in the office. Nevertheless, do not hesitate to use suitable men in the office.

As can be seen, the job of the volunteer coordinator is to see that the office is kept staffed, a very responsible position.

ii.   FIELD VOLUNTEERS

Besides the telephone or front-line women, we have back-stage women whom we call field volunteers. These women are supposed to meet with the girls, if needed, or be available to talk to girls on their home telephone. Even if a woman, because of family commitments, cannot keep office hours, she can give an invaluable service by speaking to a girl for an hour or so by telephone at home. We have several of these women to whom we owe a great deal. Some are able to drive girls for appointments with doctors or prospective employers or find accommodation for them. Occasionally, a girl from out of town must be met at a railway or bus station or in a hotel room. In these cases we ask the women to be accompanied by another person, always, unless she knows the girl. Some volunteers do clerical work and typing. Another is responsible for all copying, another for the layettes and maternity clothes.

Our experience has shown that it is best to have the telephone volunteers call me when in need of a co-worker. Of course, someone else could do this job also, but I find that I want to do this, and in this way I am in touch with the entire staff. I know all the cases in detail personally, and I am able to direct the girls to the second volunteer who can be of most help to her. For example, a volunteer with a small baby herself, cannot leave everything at a moment's notice and meet a desperate girl. I know the women and their capabilities and responsibilities. This is the executive director's job, at least, for the present time in this Birthright centre. If necessary, I can fill in myself and occasionally want to do this. I am never so happy in this work as when dealing directly with girls, and it is to my sorrow, that I have so little time for this now.

iii. MEDICAL APPOINTMENTS

In order that there be no overlapping, all medical appointments should be made through the woman in charge of these, and a volunteer, here, is doing a good job. We have over twenty-five doctors who have offered their services and it is important that there be a record kept of appointments. Nevertheless, it may be unnecessary for a smaller Birthright operation to have this type of coordination.

It is important here to clarify that our doctors do not offer *free* medical care. To do this would be to leave ourselves open for exploitation. What this does mean is that these doctors, being familiar with and sympathetic to our work, will see a distressed pregnant girl as soon as possible, if necessary, sometimes even immediately. This is important and a large contribution, since, in this area at least, it is next to impossible to get a doctor's appointment, and certainly not in short notice. Of course, many of our doctors do give some free medical care, if indicated, and necessary. However, we do have free obstetrical clinics, and at St. Michael's Hospital our girls are given special attention and appointments. A word of warning here. Some clinics readily give abortions and we cannot use their services except in late pregnancy.

In Ontario we have a provincial medical plan, and a girl qualifies for medical care, if enrolled for at least a period of three months. The same is true of hospital insurance and often it is simply a matter of advising and helping a girl to fill out these application forms, if she has not already done so. It is the responsibility of the volunteer to find out if the girl has coverage and advise her, if not.

If a girl, for some reasons, delays here or cannot enrol, we usually help her to come to make an appointment at the free medical clinics.

Again I will mention that in exceptional cases our doctors have examined troubled penniless girls to confirm the pregnancies, without recompense and one doctor has delivered without charge at times. Perhaps, in areas where medical and hospital insurance is not available, doctors could be persuaded to deliver at a lower fee.

iv.   PSYCHIATRIC CARE

Although not often, we have found it necessary, as mentioned before, to obtain immediate psychiatric care for a girl when she seemed on the point of suicide. This can be done here through the hospital clinics or Clarke Institute of Psychiatry, or our own psychiatrist in Birthright. However, this is not a common problem. A girl's own doctor is the best judge of this and will not hesitate to obtain psychiatric help for a girl who needs it. So this is rarely the responsibility of a volunteer.

We have had some experience with very disturbed girls, suffering from paranoia and schizophrenia. These, we have found necessarily, must be given over to the professional. One poor girl, seven months pregnant, was helped in every capacity, finding her accommodation, employment and medical care. The volunteer spent hours with her, driving her around. It was only after days of disturbing situations, including an incident when the girl called me to accuse the volunteer of stealing money from her, that we

50

learned she had been under psychiatric care for paranoia. As soon as we knew this, we left her to the professionals who placed her in the hospital, under observation, until she delivered.

Another disturbed girl phoned to tell us she was pregnant by the celibate clergyman in her local parish. For a month I listened to her daily, suspecting her story to be a fabrication, and yet, because she sounded so plausible and because she kept threatening to have an abortion, I went on with her. Gradually, by carefully checking some of her stories, I realized that none of them were true. Also, all the girls who need us, eventually reveal themselves to us, because they come to trust us; but she never did. Her moods varied, sometimes abusive, sometimes tearful, and there was some instinct that told me she might be a pathological case. When I became sure of this, I told her very firmly, yet kindly, not to call again, and for her own sake, to obtain psychiatric help. It was a relief to close the case.

v.   PAY HOMES

If a girl needs a home, and is also without money, we have a long list of private homes available. One volunteer is in charge of these. When we opened office and were given some publicity, we were flooded with calls, offering homes. Soon we realized that, although a few of these people were motivated by charity, many were more interested in obtaining cheap domestic help. The fact is that they seemed to think of Birthright as a domestic employment agency.

So it became necessary, for the protection of the girls, to screen the homes and to lay down some rules governing placement. One woman called asking for a girl to "baby-sit" her two dogs while she went to business. We certainly are not in the "dog-sitting" business.

The girl must have a room of her own and as much privacy as possible. She should have one full day and also one half-day a week off, and a rest period in the afternoons. There should be no heavy cleaning, just light duties and baby-sitting. The mother should not go to work, nor leave the girl alone with the children for long periods, that is for trips to hospital, or elsewhere. The rate of pay can vary according to the area.

Nevertheless, the fact is that we have found that the majority of girls we help do not wish to go into these homes. They find the idea of domestic work distasteful and will do this only when necessary. Business girls usually can continue to work, but nurses often must leave their positions when pregnancy occurs. Many of these are willing to go into a pay home and do very well.

We have, by now, several good homes on our list, but have written a few off. Girls should not be treated as servants and the people we find most suitable are concerned for the girl, and will take her in as a member of the family. Then she is happy and these people can be a tremendous support to a girl. Some homes have now had several of our girls, one after another, and it is a very happy situation.

When we have found a home to be suitable, when the girl is left freedom to be herself in order to make her own decisions as to adoption and medical care, we are willing then to place other girls in the home. We found the woman in one home discouraging the girls from going to the Children's Aid Society and found she was arranging for private adoptions. We never used her home again.

So, one word of warning here! We found that some people were putting pressure on the girls towards private adoptions, and this looked, suspiciously, as if a "black market" was operating in this area. We now, for the protection of the girls, accompany them to the Children's Aid Society, the adoptive agencies in Toronto, for counsel and legal adoption procedure and refuse to place our girls in any home we suspect.

vi.   MATERNITY HOMES

One volunteer also looks after this. There are six maternity homes in this area; all of them denominational. Although at first most of them were filled to capacity and had long waiting lists, now, because of the increase in abortions, there are many vacancies. For the younger pregnant girls, the maternity homes offer the best solution if they wish to continue their high school education and we encourage the girls to go to them. At first, we found it possible to get our girls into these homes, if not one, perhaps another, when needed, because of cancellations and unexpected premature deliveries. For some, this is not the best answer, but for others it is the most practical solution. So much real help is given, in therapy and counselling. However, today, the maternity homes are, often, only partially filled and perhaps this kind of help to pregnant girls may be becoming obsolete. Certainly their re-assessment is needed.

vii.   ACCOMODATION

If a girl needs a room, the volunteer helps here. Generally, we have a few people listed who will give, at least, temporary accommodation. It is difficult for a pregnant girl to ask, through classified advertising, for accommodation. One girl told us that she had called 34 rooming homes and each time she was refused when she revealed her condition. She had begun to feel rather desperate when she called us. A volunteer took over the search for her, and came up with a very nice accommodation. Nothing is impossible in Birthright it seems.

Here I'd like to tell the story of Giselle, a very sweet little French Canadian. One of her field volunteers had been to Sunday Mass at Newman Chapel and she asked the priest to allow her to make an appeal for accommodation. She had some offers right there. Then the next morning a call came from a University student, who said he was leaving on May 31st for a month's stay in London to work on his thesis. He offered us free use of his apartment. We met him and obtained the key before he left. It was a third floor "walk-up," a charming bachelor's den, tastefully furnished. I loved it. His one request was that his petunias in the window box be watered.

On the evening of May 31st, Giselle, for the first time, called the office saying that her baby, two weeks overdue, had not arrived and that she must move the next day. (She had given notice, believing the baby would have come and she could go home to Quebec by the end of the month.) I promised to take her to the student's apartment next morning. When I arrived she was in labour, and instead, I drove her to the hospital, and little Yvonne was born two hours later. Within a week, I drove both mother and baby to the apartment and they remained there until the end of the month. From there she went home to Quebec. I shall never forget her delight in that apartment.

By this, you can see that we give help, no matter in what stage of pregnancy the girl finds herself. We are an emergency pregnancy service and we help every pregnant girl who calls on us. The fact is that, no matter who is on the other end of the telephone line, if that person is in need, we give assistance. If it is not a pregnancy case, usually we can refer the person to another distress centre. Only once did we find it necessary, to help a case other than pregnancy, because it seemed there was no one else to help, and it was the attempted suicide of a young man attending college.

Of course, there are fake and crank calls – from men and girls. Strangely, most "fake" calls come from men who will try to have us call girls, giving us their number. We are now alerted to these, and can tell the difference. In *every* instance when a man has called asking us to call his girlfriend or sister in order to help her, we have found it to be a "fake" call. At first we would call the number, carefully sounding out the girl, if she were authentic, to learn that there was no pregnancy. Of course, we always explained and apologized. Now, always, when a man calls, we ask that we have the girl, herself, call us, and this has seemed to eliminate, almost entirely, the problem.

Just recently, I answered the phone at our Campus office and a masculine voice, disguised to sound somewhat feminine, said:

"Can you help me?"

"In what way?" I said.

"In what way can you help me? I am pregnant."

"How do you know that?

"How does one usually tell? I just know I am."

"Then tell me your problems and I'll see what I can do."

"I am so embarrassed."

"I should think it would be embarrassing for a boy to be pregnant."

There was a burst of unmistaken male laughter and the caller hung up. So there are amusing incidents in Birthright. That one made my day, after one or two real distress calls.

This does not mean that all calls from men are not genuine. Most are, in fact, and they are very sincere in wanting help or in finding information for a girl friend, a sister or a daughter. However, these men never ask us to call the girls, but will, instead, urge the girls to call us. Sometimes, they will bring the girls to us, and we find fathers of pregnant girls very grateful for our help here.

One really distressed call came from a young man of sixteen who was disturbed over an unwanted pregnancy – unwanted on his part – his mother's. He was an only child and his mother was pregnant. She was so delighted she spoke of nothing but the coming child. Since he was genuinely unhappy we talked to him, and encouraged him to speak about it to his mother who would understand.

When we receive very obscene phone calls we hang up. If repeated, we threaten to ask help from the telephone company. This usually works. Always, if there seems to be a mental disturbance, we refer to the Clarke Institute of Psychiatry as charitably as possible. These calls must be dealt with quickly to free the lines for genuine calls. Women, as well as men, can be the callers here and usually in the case of women, there seems to be a problem of lesbianism.

viii.   EMPLOYMENT

I have already explained the pay homes which take care of both accommodation and employment. However, business girls generally wish to continue working in offices. Nevertheless, they are embarrassed when their condition begins to show, and many will not remain in the same position. So we have contacted the office placement services and found them most co-operative. In fact, one of them stated that they liked hiring pregnant girls as they were very reliable.

These agencies informed us that they do not care about the marital or maternal status of a girl, if she is neat and can do the work. She is to wear a wedding ring, and be addressed as "Mrs." Her employers will be told that she will arrive wearing maternity clothes. The girls tell us that they find this arrangement very satisfactory and they are able to work until the baby is almost due.

ix.   OUT-OF-TOWN ARRANGEMENTS

We have found it possible to make contact in almost any city for a girl who wishes to leave town by calling parish priests or friends. So we have sent girls to Vancouver, Scotland and various parts of Ontario. Pay homes, maternity homes or room and board can usually be found in other areas, and now all that is to be needed is to call the closest Birthright centre in Canada or the United States. Soon, there will be a chain of these from coast to coast.

x.   MATERIAL AID

We do not have funds to spare for financial help for anyone, and, it has seemed advisable to follow a policy of not doing this for very obvious reasons. It could lead to exploitation. Of course, I know there are instances when a volunteer has given funds of her own. I make no effort to interfere here. I have done the same. However, we do ask for donations of maternity clothes and layettes and find we need a constant supply of these, most especially the maternity clothes for our girls. None have been refused this type of material aid and it is wonderful to see a girl's face light up when she walks out with a smart maternity dress. We also find offers of baby furniture, which are soon put to use. We make no charge for this material help.

Parish organizations here have been holding baby showers for us and the clothing is all new and beautiful. I follow a policy of never giving to an unmarried mother, for her baby, what I would not have put on my own baby.

xi.   UNDER-AGE TEENAGERS

In the beginning it was very rare for girls under sixteen to come to us. Last week we had four and the number is increasing. When they do, we urge them to tell their parents immediately so that the problem can be solved in the home. If the case becomes known to authorities, the boy can be charged, if old enough, with carnal knowledge (statutory rape) if the parents wish to press the charge. Most do not.

Birthright would never report these cases, although one agency told me that we *must*. The fact is that we pledge complete secrecy to the girls and we cannot break this pledge for any reason or no matter how young the girl. This is of the greatest importance for the image of Birthright, as well as the protection of the girls, who *always come first*.

As you can see, we do have a system, yet there is flexibility. No rule is ever made "hard and fast." For example: if the medical coordinator is not immediately available to get a medical appointment for a girl, we would go ahead, on our own, if it were imperative to do so. We must be permitted to use initiative and responsibility and a loose structure permits this.

I recall a meeting we had, just a few days before opening. The women had been through the training course, and some of them at the teach-in in June. In other words, we had been given a basic training in counselling and courteous answering, and a knowledge of the abortion problem. Yet there was a great anxiety. Some of the committee were sure that more test cases should have been given.

For myself, I was not concerned. I believe we must avoid stereotyped answers and for this reason I had refused to give "practice answering" instructions. Finally, I said: "All of us are here for a single purpose; to help girls in distress. Even as we are united in this aim, all of us are different, each with her own special talent to give. Every situation will be different, and each of us will approach it in our own special way. The Holy Spirit is the one who will guide us. So just relax, and let Him take over and inspire you, when you pick up the phone."

That is exactly how it went. There have been very few problems. No trained volunteer has been requested to leave Birthright. There have been a few who left, openly, honestly, saying it was just not for them, or because of other commitments. We now have a wonderful core group doing outstanding work and each fall brings another group ready to train. After an appeal in the parish bulletins for volunteers in late September, we usually add a few more treasured people to our lists. The average seems to be about twenty percent success from the people who register as volunteers.

xii.   BIRTHRIGHT COFFEE DATE

An outline of our services would be incomplete without telling you of our drop-in centre. The story of this is, that, in October 1969, I received a phone call from a woman, Vi Mackintosh, saying that she felt very called to help the girls and that she would like to have a "drop-in" centre for them one day a week. I asked her if she could, with the help of two or three other volunteers, operate it alone, as I was so busy. After ensuring me of this, she told me of her plans. She would approach her local church pastor and ask for the use of a large room. Her idea was to keep this an entirely social affair, that is, free of all discussion of problems. She would teach the girls to sew, knit and crochet, if they wished, and serve, coffee, tea and cookies. Now Birthright Coffee Date, every Wednesday afternoon, has been in operation for three years, going from October until June. I attend personally, on special occasions, that is for parties for Christmas, Valentine, etc., and I am always thrilled to see the results of Vi's efforts. We had two sewing machines donated, and it is really gratifying to see a pregnant teenager happily working on a new maternity outfit, or a dress she can wear later on. Those keeping their babies, may be crocheting a little bonnet, or smocking a baby nightie.

Sister Mary Candon helps Vi operate the centre and her long years of experience as a teacher in a girls' school is invaluable, not only here, but in her other two shifts as a telephone volunteer. We have, by the way, four sisters now helping in a volunteer capacity and they are really outstanding in the dedication and love they give to this work. I hope all centres will not hesitate to request sisters as volunteers. Many, as we women know from experience, have a "built-in" maternal instinct, and this, along with years of helping girls, and their training and dedication make them among our best volunteers. Also, we find that, although the girls, both Catholic and Protestant, eventually know that these are sisters, there is no embarrassment or reluctance. This proves that when a distressed girl needs help, it matters little from whom the help comes. What she needs is someone who cares.

The fact is, now, that not only in Toronto, but in other areas of North America, Birthright has become well-known and very well accepted in the community. Rarely a week passes here, in Toronto, without an offer of financial and volunteer assistance. Not only that, we are seeing that, out of our personal sacrifices, in helping with the personal tragedies in the lives of those who come to us, that the minds and hearts of people are being enlightened, educated and changed. There is still much goodness in people, and we must not forget that God is very real, and that, as the Creator of Life, He is far more concerned for the babies He creates than we are, as great as our concern is. In Birthright, He is showing that the solution to unwanted babies is to help, not abort.

6. AIMS AND OBJECTIVES

"To uphold, at all times, that any pregnant girl or woman has the right to whatever help she may need to carry her child to term, and to foster respect for human life at all stages of development."

This is the creed and philosophy of Birthright. Those of us who work in Birthright have learned that there are people who do not believe every mother has the right to bring her child into the world. Even some zealous Christians will debate this point, saying that an unwanted pregnancy is not our responsibility, and that a girl has no right to give birth to a child out of wedlock. These people may not, perhaps, advocate wholesale abortion: but they frown on any positive action to prevent it.

People who think like this, and profess to be Christians, would do well to re-examine their thinking. They might ask themselves if they are truly following Christianity as taught by Jesus, or a counterfeit, hypocritical, pharisaical Christianity.

This attitude is, in reality, a product of a moralistic deformation of the Christian message. The false shame which presents sexuality in its entirety as culpable is still widespread today; and many people believe it to be biblical in origin. In reality, the Bible speaks of sexuality with simplicity and realism. One time, a friend, a good Christian, intimated in a lengthy discussion that she thought unmarried girls are being encouraged in their "wrongdoing" by our helping them. "How is it possible," she said, "that you can condone actions contrary to the laws of God?"

I answered, "How much wrongdoing can you or I say is involved? Also, are we to help only sinless people? We are all forgiven sinners. If we are to start eliminating sinners, then I must start with myself." Did not David say: "I have gone astray like a lost sheep. Seek Your servant...?" (Psalm 119, 176)

Later this friend phoned me: "You're right. Thanks for showing me how hypocritical my thinking was." So there it is! I esteem this woman who is sincere and far from pharisaical. However, moralism is more apt to creep into the thinking of Christians who are most careful of their own moral conduct. All of us must guard against this. When moralism is present, the breath of the Spirit is stifled, and we tend to judge people not as God sees them but by our own merciless standards. Only if we try to understand the greatness of God and His love are we able to push aside pettiness and become merciful. "He delights in Mercy," (Micah 7: 18).

At one time, it was common to explain illegitimacy on the basis of congenital weakness of character, mental deficiency and immorality. Today, we are examining individual emotional and environmental factors which can contribute to pregnancy in the unmarried teenager and older girl. Moralism must give way to understanding and help.

There is no single factor to account for all instances of pregnancy out of wedlock. Only after gaining an appreciation of all the multiple factors involved can we begin to deal intelligently with the problem. There is no single, simple solution. A girl may become pregnant by intention, by accident or with no intent.

Birthright volunteers try to have an understanding of the problems of the girls. There has been a great deal of research done on the subject of unmarried mothers and this can benefit us greatly. It also can help us to maintain our own non-judgment, and influence the thinking of the community. In order to do this we take a personal interest in the girl and her well-being, and try to have an appreciation of her specific needs. We also make appropriate use of community resources.

Parents can be assisted to understand their daughters. Many mothers, and a few fathers, ask our help to obtain abortions for their daughters, even though the girls themselves want to continue with their pregnancies. One girl came to us in her third pregnancy. She was only seventeen, and her first two pregnancies had been terminated by illegal abortions, arranged by her mother. Now she was pregnant again, and she had come to Birthright because she wanted us to help her to have the child. We managed to obtain counselling for her and her mother through Family Services.

Teenage pregnancy often points to deeper personal problems. In these instances, abortion, rather than solving the problems, aggravates them. In cases like this, parents need to be shown that repeated pregnancy in a young girl is often indicative of underlying psychological or environmental conditions which abortion will never cure. The fact is that the true needs of any pregnant girl or woman cannot be met by making it possible for her to empty her womb.

What is needed is an increased interchange of knowledge and better communication, and an involvement of the whole community. Birthright volunteers can and do often become a liaison between doctors, social workers, clergy and parents. However, our main objective is to meet the greatest need, that is, of a truly loving, dedicated and compassionate service. Already we are seeing far-reaching effects of our work.

Man has been so proud of his technical, cultural and economic achievements; and in some instances has believed that he has no further need of God. Now we find our society is crumbling. There are social and political upheavals all over the world, revolt and revenge by the outcasts of society.

There is a crisis of values which creates a paradoxical situation. Young people who comprise our future adult society often live a life with material comforts never before known to man, but, on the other hand, with a dearth of meaning, of direction, or clear and definite purpose.

The crisis of values is not always recognized, because we are part of it. And this makes it difficult to see the family in its proper perspective, that is, as the centre of the scheme of things. Therefore, in spite of the marvelous advances in education and in community help for people in trouble, they still fall far short of fulfilling the greatest need – genuine love and concern for others as persons. Some individual social workers and teachers do place value on these things; but, for the most part, society is concerned with other things.

As was said by Charles Hauter, a theologian: "It is by becoming persons ourselves that we discover the persons of our fellow men." For the Christian, becoming a person means a life of contact and dialogue with God, which leads to contact and dialogue with other people.

The more a girl opens her heart to me, the more important it is that she finds in me a person in close contact with God, even though I do not speak of God to her. Only love can bring about the true understanding needed in spiritual communion with another person. And where love is, God is. Information is intellectual, but communion is spiritual. Although we need information to achieve communion, it is only through communion that we understand people, not as cases, but as persons. When we have established a communion of love with a girl, only then are we each able to show ourselves as we are, without acting a part, playing a role.

When we give our love to a lonely, downcast girl, a victim of the cruelty of people and circumstances, we, whether we believe it or not, are the instruments of the restorative power of God; for Jesus said, "Whoever does the will of my Father in heaven, is my brother, and sister, and mother." (Matthew 13: 50) Perhaps this girl has never met anyone so keenly interested in her, who listens with so much attention, who seeks to understand without judging, who, far from showing contempt, displays real respect for her as a person. In Birthright, she finds security and the consciousness of her value as a woman – a true reflection of the esteem of God.

In our counselling role in Birthright there is no need to plunge into religious and philosophical theories about life, man or God. Often we can help most if we just listen to the girl, in silence. If we believe that we can help people by indoctrination, denunciation, in moral uplift, or by exhorting them to pray, we will be far wide of the mark, and will be attempting a function which does not belong to Birthright. Our need is to have an unconditional respect for the girl, and to ask God to guide us in helping her.

Our philosophy, and clear-cut duty, is to bear witness to the truth that all human life is sacred. Much has been said about the rights of the unborn child. One of the dangers of this age which puts such a premium on science and technology is that we become impersonal and see people as automata, as robots. This can cause a total disregard for the dignity of human life.

We need to realize that life, liberty and the person are not phenomena, but a compelling and sacred experience, calling for recognition. Because we tend to de-humanize and de-personalize, we place little value on the fetus. Birthright upholds the right of the fetus to be born. By doing this we are prophetically protecting the whole idea of the sanctity of human life in an age when man is gaining more and more power over life.

The crux of the abortion problem is the unwanted child; and yet it is our society which has created the conditions that make a child unwanted. So these conditions can be changed! We do not have to accept them. We speak so lightly of unwanted children and the problems surrounding them. And rather than correct our socio-economic failures and shortcomings, we seek means of eliminating the children before they come into our midst. It is our society which puts a label on who is unwanted, not the mother.

When Birthright first went into operation in October 1968, most abortions being performed in Canada were illegal, done on back streets. Now, with the liberal law, allowing abortions legally, for reasons of mental and physical health, hundreds of girls and women are being aborted in our hospitals, and for socio-economic reasons. Hundreds more are going across the border to New York State. Also, contrary to what many believe, the back-room operator is still very much in business. Although medical insurance pays for hospital abortions, there are hundreds of girls and women still seeking out the back-room abortionist, and there always will be, for the sake of secrecy and expediency. There is one difference, the price has gone down. Recently, one of our girls informed us of a woman who was performing abortions for $25 and was doing a thriving business. The girl who informed us became frightened after arranging an abortion, and came to us for help to have the child.

The cry that abortion on demand will eliminate back-room operators is far from true and has been proven false by the experiences of other countries with liberal laws. Abortion on demand has been legal in Japan since 1949 and yet, according to statistics, the illegal abortion rate is almost as high as the legal. Also, Japan has now reached a crisis situation. She is a country of elderly people, and faces a labour shortage. If Japan is to survive, from committing genocide, she must take action soon against this wholesale slaughter of her unborn future citizens. The effects on the mental health of the women have been drastic. However, it seems that the attitudes are changing in that, while families of more than two children have been suffering great hardships being socially unaccepted and unable to find suitable accommodation, now the trend is towards larger families again. There is now hope for the future of Japan.

We are aware that, compared to the great number of abortions performed, Birthright seems to be merely "skimming the surface." Nevertheless, we are saving hundreds of human lives and our work is spreading quickly. In Birthright, inspired people swing into action, and here is a cause to challenge concerned citizens everywhere, the beautiful sight of lovely young women with their babies, alive and very much loved and wanted.

The truth is, that, in Birthright, we are proving that abortion need not be the way of the future. There are other ways to cope with the problems we face and these ways are preferable, not because they are quicker and lazier, but because they sow respect for people as they really are, for the sexual act in all its implications, for parenthood and the family.

By being easily accessible by telephone, girls and women, with unwanted pregnancies, whose first impulse is to seek abortions, are able to find instead concerned people who can help them to take stock of the situation and consider the alternative solutions. A Birthright program cannot flourish without dedicated people. It is a question of whether our values are firm enough and our compassion is strong enough.

7.   THE VOLUNTEERS

An abortion epidemic has invaded the world as, country after country, and state after state are making legal the destruction of unborn human life. Rev. Anthony Zimmerman, an expert on population problems, has warned us to watch the statistics on illegal abortions. He claims that the real danger exists, not so much in making legal an insignificant number of therapeutic abortions, but that some day, illegal operations may no longer be prosecuted. This is of vital interest to us.

Birthright offers a challenge and an opportunity. With millions of lives in danger there is a great need for women who will take the responsibility, who can think for distressed humanity – and not just for themselves. The problems of our times, the problems of unwed mothers and unwanted children demand, on the part of women, and men also, as never before, a sense of responsibility, moral strength and a spirit of sacrifice.

Six months before opening office, I appealed, in the only way it seemed available, through the parish bulletins, for volunteers. The response was good, ninety women telephoned me. I outlined our plan to them, promising a meeting before long, and a course of instruction. On consultation with a committee of clergy, we decided on a full day Teach-in as suggested by one priest who offered the parish hall for this purpose. We "scouted" around for speakers and were surprised and gratified by the response. In June we held the concentrated course which started on a Friday evening, and went on all day Saturday. The speakers were comprised of doctors, social workers and Catholic and Protestant clergy. About 60 volunteers came and we considered it to be a wonderful success. There were box lunches prepared by some of the women. (Now, at our full day training sessions to eliminate this work, volunteers bring their own lunches, and tea and coffee is served.) Of course, after that summer came, and little could be done. I caught up on a back-log of correspondence, made plans, and filled out forms for Income Tax Exemption.

In September, another course was planned for six evenings, two a week for three weeks. Again the community quickly supplied generous speakers – a professor of psychology, and experienced counsellor; Detective Douglas Walton of the Morality Bureau, an expert on the problems of illegal abortions; a gynecologist, who has made a study on the subject of abortion; two other doctors, experienced with unwed mothers; the Bell Telephone Company, and social worker for the Children's Aid Society. Included in the program was the showing of films, one especially pertaining to the different stages of the unborn child, and also "Phoebe," borrowed from the National Film Board. (We recommend this film.)

By the end of the course, the women had become acquainted with each other and bonds of friendship and love were established. They are a wonderful group and it is a privilege, on my part, to have them in Birthright as co-workers. Their dedication to Birthright and their loyalty to me, personally, is a great source of inspiration and encouragement to me. The fact is that the great spirit of love which activates our group is outstanding and an inspiration to many.

Since opening, some volunteers have left, for various valid reasons, and there will always be a turnover, I am sure. However, the majority are still with us and from time to time, women call us offering their services. Always, we question these, because quite often they misinterpret our aims, and, if these women do not agree with our basic philosophy, of course they do not belong with us. If they do join Birthright, we have them into the office for training. Then when a course is offered, such as the Teach-in in February or a lecture at the Police Headquarters, they are expected to attend. We always have an on-going learning process and along with the increase of knowledge is the opportunity to meet in a group socially which is important.

Recently the Chairman of the Department of Adult Education, Dr. Alan Thomas, said that volunteer agencies must re-think their goals and their structure if they are to remain influential and effective. He told the 1972 Assembly of Canadian Voluntary Health Agencies that no voluntary organization which expects to educate the public can succeed or survive if it does not educate its own members or at least permit and encourage them to learn. Volunteers give time and energy in the expectation that their contribution is valued, that they can take some part in allocation of resources and be able to see the consequences.

Dr. Thomas said that, "While honouring and manipulating the volunteer, we have despised and been contemptuous of the amateur, branding him as little more than a well-meaning incompetent. Yet the volunteer and the amateur are one, and this view is painfully and vigorously corrected now."

He stated that conferences held by voluntary bodies produced impressive achievements. Their deliberations on ecology, education and many other areas are of great value.

There is little doubt that Birthright could qualify as a voluntary group which has produced, and continues to do so, very impressive achievements. Nevertheless, it is important to keep in mind the advice of Dr. Thomas, that we should keep informed, study, read and have a continuing learning program, if we are to remain effective.

Truly, I cannot praise too highly our group of wonderful women, and now, we also have some men. We are learning that because we share a common impulse to save lives, we are living the life of the Spirit more deeply, by going out to people in distress, and we are also finding God in each other.

There are the women working in a secretarial capacity. One in particular who I think, drops everything else to get work out for me. Also, there is one volunteer, who, in the fall, manages to contact all the high school principals and guidance counsellors, explaining our work. Because of this, we had some of the principals ask for our help with girls. Two volunteers go to the office, once weekly, to houseclean it, and for a long time I had no knowledge of this. Humility such as this shows me how little I have of it.

The fact is that if Birthright has been "put on the map" in this area and become a real public service, and there are no doubts about this, it has been through the co-operative efforts and sacrifices of this group of heroic women, and men. I hope the Birthright centres starting up in other areas will be as fortunate as we have been. Since God is our guide, no doubt they will.

Birthright has a divine purpose, the saving of human life in this abortion age, and God is calling us to fulfill this purpose, and at the same time fulfill our own personal destiny. Birthright is "truth in action" and, as we look back over the road we have travelled, we can see the guiding force is the Creator of life who leads us, in spite of every deviation and human weakness.

Birthright can become for some women, a vocation. Cardinal Duvas read a message to women at the Vatican Council. Part of this reads: "You women have always had, as your lot, the protection of the home, the love of beginnings, the understanding of cradles… You are present in the mystery of a life beginning. You offer consolation in the departure at death. Our technology runs the risk of becoming inhuman. Reconcile men with life and above all, we beseech you, watch carefully over the future of our race. Hold back the hand of men who, in a moment of folly, might attempt to destroy human civilization."

To be involved in Birthright means living, in very truth, creatively, because we are taking part, with God, in the very act of creation. Membership in Birthright, as a volunteer, is a free response to the Spirit in which we seek to understand our own gifts, and bring them forth to share them with others. We choose to deepen our commitment to the Spirit, through deepening our commitment to others. It is difficult because it demands self-revelation which is the very thing we all find so threatening. At the same time we hunger to share with others, and alienation and loneliness are the prices we pay when we are unwilling, or incapable, of giving up the defenses that shut us off from other people.

The first act of a Birthright group is one of trust, trust of each in all, and this is a growing trust. It is here that the director is needed in the way she complements this with the openness of her own personality, of her readiness for friendship and growth with others.

The task of the Birthright director is not to dominate but, through her own person, unite. The process of growth in relationship to each other with the director as the core of the group's development is not an easy one. Masks and facades must be dropped or the group never gets anywhere. This is a very intense and demanding process. There needs to be understanding and acceptance of one another.

It is as a Birthright group grows and encounters difficulties and works them through, that it begins to develop a sense of its identification as a part of this whole international movement. We are then called to move beyond the point of existing solely for our mutual support and common goal, and become apostolic in a full and vigorous sense, and this is inevitable, if activities are truly motivated by the Holy Spirit. The Birthright Founding Office is then the dynamic centre; the focus for continuing this great and rewarding work with mothers and babies. If we seek to over-organize and superstructure internationally with committees and elections, much will be lost. We must strive vigorously to put down any tendency to become a large insensitive bureaucratic international organization. We are not a democratic organization, as some would make us, but rather, a spiritual and apostolic movement explainable only in the light of God's grace.

8. THE DOCTORS

Many doctors, and especially gynecologists, disapprove of abortion and it has not been difficult to find, in this area, many who are willing to help in Birthright. They see in this a positive means of combating the terrible scourge of the abortionists, while at the same time, helping distressed pregnant women. The truth is that the response of the doctors has been most gratifying. They have welcomed distressed girls indiscriminately, and in all their diversity, not only giving them technical medical help, but what is more important, support in their suffering, torment and conflict.

As explained before, I spent many months in the planning before officially opening office. By telephone, I contacted doctors in different areas, making certain that they would share our basic philosophy. I would call them, explain our objectives, send literature to them and, after a week or so, again contact them. Of all the doctors called, there was only one refusal. Perhaps some were rather tentative about their offer to help, but at least they did not say "No." By the time we opened, twenty doctors and one psychiatrist had offered to be on call, and they are now increased to 26.

Of course, some of those doctors had been greatly involved from the start. One doctor, having made a study of abortion, has also been actively involved in our training program, so too, another, who is a pediatrician, has had much experience with unwed mothers.

Before opening, I used to wonder if we really had enough doctors available, only to find that we do not make use of them to the extent we expected. We have given help to hundreds of girls in the first four years of operation, but we do not, of course, have a continuing responsibility to all of these. Also, many girls decide to go to doctors of their own choice once they agree to go through with the pregnancy. A great many, because of financial reasons, attend the hospital clinics.

Some doctors have been consulted more often than others because of their location. Central locations are more readily available for girls going to business. Because of this, we have been asked, at times, for appointments with other than Birthright doctors and found no difficulty in obtaining these appointments. Our public image is very good and becomes more so as word of our loving acceptance and practical assistance to mothers and their babies spreads.

Although here, in Canada, we do not often send a girl to a doctor unless she has her medical insurance, or is able to get it, we do not feel we can, in fairness, expect one doctor to take on too many girls. All are busy. For this reason, the medical appointments must be coordinated, and one volunteer, guides the volunteer in the choice of a doctor for a girl, taking into consideration the location of her home, and the hospital she wishes to enter, as well as the number of girls already sent to the doctor.

We do not, indiscriminately, give our doctors' names over the telephone. We have this type of request, that a person will call and ask for the name of our doctors as she cannot get a doctor's appointment. Since there is usually no question here of a distressed pregnancy, but just of convenience, we usually refer these cases to the Academy of Medicine. This is another good reason for having one volunteer in charge of the medical appointments. Certainly, concrete help can be given if a girl comes into the office for an interview and we make the first appointment for her.

What is most important, and illuminating, is the way our doctors are understanding the need of integrative medicine in handling the girls. These girls tell us how very kindly the doctors treat them, taking into consideration the whole problem of the girls, assisting them, not only technically, but psychologically and also spiritually, and how these guilt-ridden girls need this!

Not long ago, Marnie, 21, a college student, called me at the office, and she was fully determined to have an abortion. She was six weeks pregnant and the pregnancy had been confirmed just the day before. Her distress was extreme to the point of hysteria, and it took several moments to calm her. She did not want to take a chance with an abortion in New York State, but hoped, some way, a qualified practitioner could be persuaded to abort her.

I explained to her, what few girls realize, how dangerous even hospital abortions are. People in general think that if an abortion is done by a gynecologist, in a good hospital, then all danger is eliminated. Yet in January 1971, the chief gynecologist of Toronto General Hospital, Dr. Edward Harkins, in an article in "The Toronto General Monitor," clearly stated that abortion is a very dangerous operation. The fact is that, over the past year, there have been enough deaths from abortions done in hospitals in Toronto to cause the chief coroner to warn the public of the dangers. One 21-year-old unmarried girl died several days after a saline injection. This has shocked many people, thank God, making them take abortions seriously.

Of course, in speaking to Marnie, I did not go into details like this, just simply warned her of the danger of abortion and offered to get her an appointment with one of our doctors. She went to him that same afternoon.

That evening she called me. The miracle had taken place once again as she told me how the doctor had calmed all her fears. She was now prepared to face the future, knowing that he would be there, ready to help. "I could have stayed there all day with him," she said. "He made me feel like a person again."

Not far from our office lives a girl, Linda, with her baby Heather. At four months pregnant, Linda, pressured on every side to have an abortion, arranged for one in a local hospital. Two attempts were made to abort her by the highly dangerous saline injection method. These attempts failed and Linda, having enough of the pain and upset of the entire ordeal, left the hospital, still pregnant. In desperation, she called Birthright and was sent immediately to one of our doctors. He calmed our fears, and then we placed her in a private home where she remained until Heather was born.

When the baby arrived, her family who had ostracized her, capitulated, and would not hear of the child being placed for adoption. With their help, Linda was able to keep the baby she almost destroyed. Now her daily walks often take her to the Birthright office and every Wednesday afternoon finds her at our "Drop-in" centre. Happiness is written all over her. The joy in that young mother's life is unmistakable. How I wish more doctors, and others who would like to see all unmarried girls aborted, could witness some of this peace which Birthright doctors are helping to bring into the lives of many of these girls.

We can readily realize that, in spite of attempts to keep his function technical, the doctor, imperceptibly, may pass from medical, to psychological, and even spiritual problems. In most unwed mothers, the question of guilt arises, and this demands an answer. If medicine is forbidden any spiritual reference, it can then treat only a partial aspect of the person. However, our spiritual needs are not set apart just for theologians, nor is the Holy Spirit the monopoly of the clergy, and, gratefully, many of our doctors are seeing this in treating the patients. Guilt is not just a religious problem, but also a social and a psychological problem. It cannot be taken apart. It causes great suffering to all human beings, and most especially to the unwed mother, and a doctor must be concerned with the relief of suffering.

Thus Birthright doctors are responding by treating the whole person of the girl. As in the case of Marnie, we are finding that the first visit to a doctor can completely change the attitude of a pregnant girl, from one of despair, to one of hope. Our doctors are now giving, not only sympathy, personal solicitude and encouragement, but also the peace that comes with divine grace, the fulfillment of the promise: "I will pour out my spirit on all flesh." (Joel 11: 28)

And this is the challenge in this abortion age for doctors who are giving abortions readily, and there are now many of these, to ask themselves why they are "opting out." They can no longer give the excuse of "unwanted babies." Hundreds of childless couples are hungrily waiting, in vain, for babies today. The girls themselves, if supported, will go on to deliver happily. How can any doctor, with a clear conscience, do this despicable act of wiping from existence another human being when his whole life is supposed to be a witness to the saving of life?

9.　THE CLERGY

When I think of the help given to me, personally, and to Birthright, by various members of the clergy, both Catholic and Protestant, I am deeply grateful. Without this help there would not be a "Birthright", for I could never have continued without their moral, and financial support.

Most important, have been the clergy who have worked closely in Birthright from its conception, and who, in spite of problems and conflict and tensions which were such an encumbrance at the time of birth, through all the difficult months which followed the official opening, with one exception, have never wavered in their faith, nor withdrawn their support and cooperation.

There has always been available accommodations for meetings, large or small at some church hall in a central location. Also we could always count on members of the clergy to lecture at our training programs, Rev. Dr. Graham Scott, a United Church minister, Father John Moss, an experienced counsellor, and Father Clair Yaeek, a sociologist, well-informed on the problem of abortion in Japan.

The list goes on and on, and only rarely have I encountered any resistance in helping in every way possible. One of the priests in the parish in which our office is located, Father John Weelink, is most enthusiastic about our work and is ready to meet any girl or person in need. He also is involved in training volunteers. And as for my own pastor and good friend, Father Carlo Cerrone, I can never repay him for his kindness, his sympathetic listening to my problems, his words of encouragement and his faith. For all of these, I love him dearly. Every Wednesday afternoon he allows the use of a large comfortable room off the church hall for our girls and babies for a social get-together. This is an important aspect of our work.

People say to me, "Are you a Catholic organization?" and, of course, I must answer negatively. However, if it were not for the Catholic people, clergy and laity, it would not have been possible to get underway. Within the Catholic community I found help in volunteer recruitment, financial backing, and advice, sound and practical. Being a Catholic I turned to my Catholic friends and they responded wholeheartedly. This is true all over North America. Yet there are those who would have us hide it. The truth can never harm Birthright. I must speak of this.

There has also been strong Protestant support and Rev. W. A. Smith of the Presbyterian Church of Canada was instrumental in obtaining the official moral backing of his church. At one time he visited our office and taped an interview with the purpose of obtaining some financial support for us. Although this has not come through as yet, I appreciate his concern and efforts.

The truth is really, that there have been clergy from every denomination ready and willing to cooperate in a positive way and this is proving to be true all over the United States and Canada. "Comfort, comfort my people, says your God." (Isaiah 40: 1,13)

Not too many girls ask for spiritual counselling but some need help from their own ministers, or priests, to tell their parents. Only when indicated, do we offer spiritual counselling, and it is our regret that more girls do not avail themselves of this means of grace. The words of eternal life, spoken by the Church, and expressed by a clergy who are genuinely interested, who understand, are needed by all of us today. All of us need their help to bear our burdens, to suffer our agonies, to heal our wounds. Too often we live in isolation, one from another, and this prevents us from being the free and loving servants of each other which God intends us to be.

Birthright came into being at the time in the history of the Church when the windows were opened to let some light in, the light which shows us that we must live the life of the Spirit in community, not in separation. We cannot escape one another. This is what the life of the Spirit is all about, to be truly human ourselves, serving other humans with love, because they need us. All around us there are people suffering, dying and crying for help and today, as never before, we need our clergy.

Certainly, the clergy working in Birthright have readily recognized, and accepted the tensions in our daily struggles as a sign that they are needed, that we cannot get along without them, that through them we are able to draw from the well of living water of which Our Lord spoke.

One of our priests, because of his particular connections has, many times, been really helpful to several of the girls. One of these was Kay, who drove here from New York City. She arrived unexpectedly in our first spring to investigate our service. Then two months later, she arrived, again, unexpectedly, to stay. We placed her as a mother's help in a private home and arranged for medical care. Then, one morning, she called me, afraid because she had not contacted the immigration authorities, and was in fact in Canada illegally. Knowing that there would be problems when her baby came, and also concerned that Birthright might be involved, unfavourably, with the Canadian Immigration Office, I contacted Father. He met Kay and accompanied her to the Immigration Office, and with his help, arrangements were made for her to remain in Canada for several more months. After she delivered her child, she returned to her home. She could not bear to part with her baby and her parents came for the two of them.

Some girls need help with wedding plans, and we have had several weddings, after the births of the babies. The girls have so many fears, afraid to marry, yet afraid not to marry; afraid to place the child for adoption, yet afraid to keep it; afraid of the social stigma of parents, friends, and employers; afraid of the loneliness, of the pains of childbirth, and of the long wakeful nights of darkness and despair, and heartbreak, and guilt; afraid, sometimes, to live any longer.

Pardon and grace produce joy, relaxation and maturity, and it is in this area that our clergy are needed most of all in helping the girls. "Gospel" means "good news" – good news of the grace of God.

However, a particularly religious approach is not necessary, as is explained by Rev. Graham Scott in one of his talks: "You must be prepared to meet them where they are in religious maturity. Remember that the other person can only trust in God as she understands Him."

And it is here we need to understand the value of the person, to know that part of Christian love is in understanding when not to speak of God, in leaving the person alone for God to speak to her. It is good to be close to people, but this closeness is healthy only when it arises spontaneously and this is the way the Spirit moves, gently, slowly and patiently. Today, we have with us a lovely young girl, and her beautiful baby, who, months after delivery, asked to be brought into the Church. It was a surprise to us because our volunteer never spoke of God to her, but it was little wonder. The beauty of the Lord shines from the eyes of this wonderful woman, a sister, fully dedicated to Birthright and our girls.

The fact is that, in Birthright, we are able to be the ideal community. In our headquarters here, we have four Sisters with us, working side by side with other women, married and single. There are no barriers between us, no thought that their religious vows or professional training put them in a separate category or require that the rest of us give them any special deference. We are one in mind and spirit, and in dedication to Birthright.

"But the word must be shown that I love the Father and do exactly as he commands." (John 14: 31) In Birthright, our clergy and our sisters are showing the world by their dedication, by their serving the needs of these pregnant girls, by their love, understanding and compassion for them, and us, the effects of the grace of God. The expression of the incarnate life of Christ must be in an active and saving love towards our neighbours. "It is by this that we know what love is, that Christ laid down His life for us and we in turn are bound to lay down our lives for others." (1 John 3: 16) Redemption has to be shared, not forced on us by fear. "There is no fear in love" (1 John 3: 16), and none either, in Birthright, where we experience trust and a sharing together of clergy, sisters and lay people.

The truth is that there have always been clergy of all denominations ready and willing to cooperate in a positive way, and through prayer. Perhaps, after all of this, the greatest help our clergy can give is through prayer for divine help. By the miracles which, daily, divine intervention plays. Many times we place down the phone after listening to a girl, wondering how we can ever find the solutions to her complex problems, and unexpectedly, perhaps, the phone will ring, and by speaking to someone we find the answer. This never fails to astonish us!

Then there are the international problems, the power struggles, so distasteful but unavoidable. In my efforts to keep Birthright from falling into the wrong hands, to preserve the non-denominational and non-structured character of Birthright, there arises the need to be strong and to take a stand when it would be so much easier to give in.

It is at times like these that I need the moral support of my friends in the priesthood, to give me courage, to let me discover God's will, and to pray with and for me. To keep Birthright unique and independent from all other organizations who want to take us under their "protective" wing, to keep us out of the hands of the people who would destroy us, is a momentous task.

And above all else, the clergy, by their presence in Birthright, are taking the opportunity not only to be active in the saving of babies' lives, but are also witnessing the sacredness of life and this leadership in regards to abortion is greatly needed in our somewhat apathetic Christian community. We need clergy in Birthright as can be seen by the following stories.

These two stories involve clergy and I think they are significant and beautiful. Just ten months ago Diane came to the Birthright office for a pregnancy test. When she found out she was pregnant, there seemed to be no way of dissuading her from having an abortion. Her mind seemed closed to any discussion of the problem, and all the solicitude of the volunteers was to no avail. She left and we thought we had failed. I have asked our women to be at peace at times like these, knowing that they have done all possible, so leave the rest to God.

We did not hear from Diane until a month ago, when the same volunteer was on duty. The phone rang.

"May I speak to Gabrielle?"

"This is Gabrielle."

"Well this is Diane. Do you remember me about ten months ago?"

"I do."

"Well I didn't have the abortion. I have a baby boy now and he's being christened tomorrow. Will you come?"

The story came out:

After leaving the Birthright office she had gone home, her mind made up. But Gabrielle's words haunted her. Also her conscience was bothering her.

She went for a walk and found herself in a church praying. A priest whom she knew came out and she hid her head hoping he would not recognize her. However he came over and spoke her name.

The whole story came out and as he listened to her, "I could feel a wonderful peace come over me," she said, "and I suddenly knew that I could never kill my baby. Although he didn't say a word, I felt that God was here and that He would help me all the way through, and He has. But you helped me too."

The next story is of a clergyman who contacted the same volunteer, because he knew her. A young woman was with him in his office. She had come because her own doctor had arranged an abortion for her the following week. She was deeply troubled because she did not really want an abortion. Gabrielle spoke to her on the phone, promising an appointment with one of our doctors as soon as possible and also our help in other ways. She now had no doubts about her decision to have the child.

What harm doctors do who, so cold-bloodedly, pronounce the death sentence on the innocent, and a lifetime of pain and heartache to their mothers. If they truly cared about people and about life, they would take the time with pregnant women, to listen and to counsel, and to find another solution other than that of destruction of the child. And here is where our clergy are needed, not only to help a girl to see that there are alternatives to abortion, but also to remind doctors that they cannot play God, and that life and death decisions must be His alone to make.

10.   COMMUNITY RESOURCES

Like so many people, before becoming involved in Birthright, I was completely uninformed about the resources in the community where people could obtain help. No doubt, every large urban centre has many of these services. Before me, now, I have the Directory of Community Services which has been compiled by the Information Service of the Social Planning Council, and this has proven to be invaluable. If starting a Birthright centre, it would be wise to investigate as to whether there is a similar directory for your area. The directory facilitates finding a required service, and makes available, by telephone, ready reference to health, welfare, accommodation, counselling, even education and prenatal classes for the expectant mothers.

The services we use most often are the Children's Aid Societies, both Catholic and Protestant. Although these agencies operate primarily for the protection of children, they offer also, casework and related services to unmarried parents. This includes adequate counselling and also arranging of adoptions.

At one of the meetings of the Board of Directors, it was decided that it would not be wise for Birthright to become involved in private adoptions, although to date, we have had several requests for babies. However, we believe it important to operate in full accord with the Child Welfare Act of Ontario. Therefore, we encourage the girls to go, as soon as possible, to the Children's Aid Societies. Now this is one of the clauses in the Birthright Charter, to leave all adoptions and adoption procedure to authorized adoption agencies.

If a girl is Jewish, she can be helped by the Jewish Family and Child Service. We have found an enthusiastic response to our work in the Jewish

Community, and this is very gratifying, although not surprising. I have always found them to be a warm and compassionate people and with fewer family problems. Although we do not have a large number of Jewish girls coming to Birthright, we do help some, and they always are very grateful.

A week after opening office, a Jewish girl, Sara, aged twenty, came to us. She was Spanish Moroccan and her family had been here for two years. In Morocco, she had been in love with a non-Jewish boy, of whom her family disapproved for religious reasons, although he was willing to convert. In Morocco, a girl must be 21 to marry without parental consent. In the summer previous to calling us, she had visited Morocco on vacation and was now three months pregnant. She was frantic because there was little hope of him being able to come to Canada before the birth of the child, because of immigration restrictions. She knew that her family would soon know of her condition, and she said she would rather abort the child than continue with the pregnancy without marriage. She even spoke of suicide.

I managed to make contact with a Jewish social worker, a tremendously kind person, and he asked me to leave it to him. Five months later I called him again about another girl. His voice was jubilant. "Mrs. Summerhill, I must tell you about Sara, the girl you sent to me. We got the wheels turning to bring the boy here. He arrived two weeks ago, they were married right away, he starts a new job next week, and the baby is due in a month." I think this is a very beautiful story.

At one time, some of the social workers seemed to believe that the Birthright volunteer, being inexperienced in counselling, might do harm to the girl. We have had no problems here, simply because we have never attempted to do her job. We offer friendship, love, and common sense in supplying the practical needs for the girls and women. We make no attempts to counsel in such areas as family problems, or whether or not the girl should marry, or whether or not she should keep her child. We need no degrees in social work, but we must be informed, and also alert in knowing when to obtain the professional counselling a girl needs.

In some parts of the United States it is not permitted for any but professional to counsel. One can see why that is when it is possible for an inexperienced person to do more harm than good. Therefore, if the volunteer makes no attempt to counsel, which must not be confused with practical advice, then there is no problem of harming the girl in any way. Birthright's function is assistance not advice. One can readily see that if a girl is being counselled by her social worker and guided in a certain direction, it would be almost disastrous for the Birthright volunteer to, in any way, interfere and thus undermine what is being done. The girl would be the person to suffer, and this would also create hostility on the part of agencies towards Birthright. For the good of the expectant mothers, cooperation between agencies and Birthright volunteers is of vital importance.

In our training of volunteers we ask the agencies to cooperate with us, and at least once a year invite some social worker from the unwed mothers' department to talk to the volunteers. This serves the dual purpose of educating the volunteer workers, and of helping the agencies understand our program. Consequently, there are few problems with social agencies in our area. The only time we part company is when a social worker advises abortion, and here is the greatest problem today.

The Children's Aid Society was founded to protect the children, born and unborn. How can advising abortion, then, ever become part of their work when it means the destruction of unborn children? In this city, there are social workers who are arranging, in cooperation with parents, all girls under sixteen to be aborted. Yet, not long ago, a report came from a leading hospital here about one third of the girls aborted in their early teens are sterilized. When I pointed this out to a social worker not long ago, she said this is good. A girl who gets pregnant in her early years may very well have repeated pregnancies, so should be sterilized. Unfortunately, this thinking is not uncommon but girls and parents should realize that, not only is this a false statement, but a completely cold and harsh one, and that it is much better to go through with a pregnancy, hard as it is, than to risk danger of sterilization.

MATERNITY HOMES

Now, for the young pregnant schoolgirl, the maternity home offers the best solution. Here she can relax with girls who share the same problem. She has medical care, her material needs are met, and she can continue her schooling. So, it is preferable to arrange all the assistance needed to carry her child to term for a young girl, rather than to arrange the destruction of her baby and possibly her own ability to have another child. All should consider carefully the positive solutions to pregnancy in a young girl other than the dangerous negative solution of abortion.

When we first opened office it was difficult at times to obtain accommodations for a girl in a maternity home. Today, because of the easy abortions, they are partly empty and not only that, they are concerned about remaining open. In the United States already many are closed. Although this could indicate a change in attitude concerning the type of help given to pregnant girls, and also that the girls themselves no longer wish to be "hidden" in this way, yet, there is a place in our society for the maternity home. Many are up-dating, allowing girls to go out to college or to work, and one in this area takes mother and baby back for a time until she is able to obtain mother's allowance and can cope as a single parent. All of these changes in maternity home care are for the better.

The unwed mother should be helped, not treated as a criminal.

FAMILY SERVICES

When a girl becomes pregnant, often the entire family must be helped to cope with the problem. Perhaps there are, even, underlying family problems which may have contributed to the pregnancy of the girl. It can deeply trouble a family, and by getting the girl, and her family, to the right service agency, the entire home can be given assistance. Especially when the girl is very young, the parents need guidance in order that their daughter be brought through the pregnancy and birth without trauma. This is the role of Birthright, to obtain help for these difficult situations and by doing so, our work can have far-reaching effects.

When needed, we refer married pregnant women to the social agency. Most often, babies are unwanted because there are marital or financial problems, and professional help is usually needed. Actually, we once had an abortion case sent to us by the Family Services, and I, personally, visited the woman in her home. The husband was pressing for an abortion, but, in time, came to accept the baby. It is true that, once the critical period is over, and the child begins to move in the womb, both parents usually adjust to the birth of another child. If help is given to straighten out the problems that make the child unwanted, the pregnancy can, very often, prove to be, even, a blessing. We have had married women call months later to tell us that life is now worth living, thanks to Birthright, and the coming child.

If an unmarried girl needs financial assistance, when she must leave her employment, we direct her to the Department of Welfare, in the area in which she lives. Her hospital and medical expenses will then, also, be covered and help will continue after the child is born until she is able to work again or obtain Mother's Allowance.

SHELTER

Although there is some emergency shelter in the community for a pregnant girl, it is not always easy to find. We, many times, have taken the girl into our own home for a day or two or longer, especially if she is in great distress. Other people have telephoned our office offering emergency shelter. We have, at times, placed a girl in the Y.W.C.A. for a night or two and although our funds are limited, the costs are not prohibitive. This is better than placing a pregnant girl in the embarrassing situation of the large free shelters run by some agencies in our city.

Regarding long-term accommodation, we often find it necessary to help by going through the classified ads with a girl. With our help, something can generally be found. I was able to find a cheap apartment for a young married woman and her family, by advising her how to obtain government housing. We simply stay with these problems until they are solved.

The fact is, that we never know, until we pick up the telephone, just where, and to whom we must turn for help, and it would seem wise for all volunteers to become familiar with the community resources in their area, even before opening office.

We have found that the agencies are accepting us, and cooperating very well. Before opening office, we met with representatives of the various agencies, most involved with the unwed mother, and also with the Social Planning Council. This has proven to be a good move. It gave them a clearer picture of what we planned to do, and what we would not, and could not do, that is, attempt to duplicate their service.

The following is a short letter a volunteer received from a caseworker of the Catholic Children's Aid Society and, I believe, it speaks for itself:

"Dear Mrs. Valin:

I enjoyed meeting you and discussing our work with you. I am enclosing some printed information which may be of interest to you.

I hope you will feel free to call me any time I can help.

> Yours sincerely,
> Ruth Cudney
> Social Worker
> Intake Department
> Children's Aid Society"

I do hope that social workers, in reading this book, will try to understand the function of Birthright, that rather than hindering the work of the agency, the volunteers in Birthright can be of great help, in performing jobs they cannot do, and providing a liaison between the girls and the agencies. The sooner distressed people are brought for help, the sooner their problems can be solved.

In our city the rapport between Birthright and the agencies is excellent, although it was not always thus in the beginnings, and even now there are a few exceptions. Also, Birthright workers should do all possible to work cooperatively with the social workers. We have much to learn from them.

11. THE MEDIA

Just after opening office, the news media learned about Birthright and got right behind us. Since this was a new type of service, and because abortion is such a controversial topic, two daily papers each gave us a very good write-up. Also two television stations came to the office and took films which they used in news broadcasts. The truth is that they all got behind us because, no matter what one's views on abortion are, no one could find fault with our loving dedication to human beings in distress.

Many however, are uncertain of our true function, think of us as an anti-abortion lobbying group, and since the media, unfortunately, are mainly pro-abortion, it is not easy to get good coverage. This is indeed unfortunate since we have found, in all Birthright centres, that, right after a newspaper article or a TV or radio interview, many girls called in for help.

The following is a letter I sent a year after opening to radio station CHUM and it explains a lot .

"September 14, 1969

Mr. Larry Wilson
CHUM Radio
Toronto

Dear Larry:

Our deepest gratitude to you and to CHUM! We thank you so very much for helping us to find little "Candy", seventeen, six months pregnant, who, hungry, bewildered and penniless, used her last dime to telephone Birthright. When we called you, you picked her up and took her home for the weekend. For this, and for all the other times, because of you, we have been able to bring peace, and help, to pregnant girls in distress, we can never forget you.

Although Birthright has proven the truth of Marshall MacLuhan's statement "the medium is the message", still the help given to us by the communication media and most especially CHUM has been tremendous.

From the start, CHUM got behind us and our first case came to us, a month before opening, because we were mentioned on a morning program. A young girl, three and a half months pregnant, had an appointment with a back-street abortionist. She heard mention of Birthright on CHUM, and being terrified, alone and penniless, she called on you for help to reach us. Within a few hours she had medical care and a place to stay. She now has a beautiful baby boy.

This is the story of the Birthright introduction to you, Larry and CHUM.

We have very little money, and cannot spend large amounts on advertising. On opening day, you gave us a tremendous boost on the news broadcast. Right after the program, *thirteen* girls called us for help.

One of these was a nineteen-year-old from Vancouver, two months pregnant. She and her boyfriend had come to Toronto in search of work. They wanted to marry, but had no money for even the license. Both came from good family backgrounds, but when I went to see them, they were living in a cockroach-infested room, in a run-down area, with another girl.

We got baby-sitting jobs for the girls, and food and clothing. Finally, the priest in the near-by church married them. One day they were evicted because they could not pay the rent. We sent then, by bus, to a northern Ontario resort, to a friend who owns a motel, and who offered to give them work. Today, they have a lovely baby boy. They are renting a little four-room house, while the father is being trained at Manpower. Three lives drastically changed by Birthright and CHUM.

Not only that, in the same house downtown, was another couple with a small baby and expecting another. We gave them a baby layette and a carriage and the moral support to go on.

From time to time, when you have mentioned Birthright on the news, we have had a flood of calls.

One of these was a young widow, 28, with five young children, and two months pregnant. The boyfriend had given her $200 for an abortion, but she was frightened. Hearing you talk about us, in desperation, she telephoned the office. We advised her to move from the area in which she was known, and enlisted the help of the St. Vincent de Paul Society. They sent volunteers to help her, and we supplied her, and the children, with clothing. Most of all, we got her much-needed medical attention and, soon, her baby will be born.

I could go on and on about the girls who came to us because of CHUM – of the young married woman, with two young children, whose husband had already contacted an abortionist. We visited her several times and got her over the 'crisis' period; – of the young girl, nine months pregnant, three days overdue, sitting alone, without money and medical care, terrified and in labour. She heard you speak of us and as soon as she telephoned we got her into the Emergency of the nearest hospital.

Then there was the case of a woman, five months pregnant, lying bleeding on the floor of her home, from an attempted abortion. She had the radio on and heard you speak of Birthright. Crawling to the phone she called us, and we rushed there and got her to the hospital. Both the mother and the baby were saved in this case, and by getting her professional counselling, her marriage problems were solved in time.

To date, Birthright, Toronto, has given some type of help to over 1 000 girls and women and many, many of these, first heard about us over CHUM.

You are doing a tremendous public service and one thing is certain, the human life saved and the hope and peace brought to these young girls and women will never be forgotten, by Birthright, nor by them.

Again, Larry, to you and to CHUM, our sincere thanks and appreciation!

Louise Summerhill
Executive Director

I never refuse interviews with reporters or to go on radio or television and this has proven to be a great means of advertising without cost. One free-lance reporter came to the office for an interview and there were articles about Birthright even in the New York Times, the Philadelphia Inquirer, the Vancouver Sun, and many others from coast to coast. We have been on the news wire service also.

It is a fact that, when reporters come into our office in an, almost, belligerent manner, sometimes only because their job required it, they have gone away completely won over by what we are doing and our loving non-judgmental and non-moralizing approach. They have pictured us as militant and strident and using aggressive anti-abortion tactics in talking to girls. When they find us to be ordinary concerned people, mothers of families, nurses or teachers, all working together in a loving dedicated service to people in distress, they cannot help but change their attitudes. The result is that, certainly, here we have had no negative articles once the writer has visited our office.

Therefore, I believe it most important to cooperate fully with the news media, and they then become our greatest means of reaching the girls in need of our service, and of putting Birthright "on the map". Some of our best friends and supporters are the newspaper, radio and television reporters, and I have found them to be very warm, human and generous in their praise of Birthright.

One reporter, a young woman working in the women's section came in to do a story. According to what she told me afterwards, she had to be "ordered" by her "boss" to come, so antagonistic and negative were her feelings about Birthright. Within an hour of listening to what we do, she was completely changed and became one of our most loyal supporters. Not only that, one pregnant girl from out of town called her after reading the article. This reporter, personally, invited her to come to Toronto, met her, then brought her to Birthright. Although she has now left this area, before doing so she had steered many girls in our direction. I felt the loss when she left town as I had come to love her. We were kindred spirits.

I think this proves that not all our enemies are cold and heartless people but are, in reality, gentle and warm and are really convinced that abortions do help the distressed girl. These people can, at times, be influenced by sincerity, love and the truth about abortion.

12. FINANCES

There have been times when I became concerned about our lack of funds, only to find that my fears were groundless. So now, when people say to me: "Where will the money come from?", I always reply: "It will come as we need it." That is the way it seems to work out. Certainly, had I waited until we had some money before beginning, there would not be a "Birthright."

When I first started, I knew enough people in the area who realized well, the sacredness of human life and who were willing to make financial sacrifices in order to save life. At this time, for them, there was as yet no question of income tax exemption, and yet, they got behind me with personal donations. In this way, I was able to take care of the initial expenses incurred with printing, stationary, postage, etc.

In the spring of 1968, I obtained the forms from the Department of National Revenue, so that we could register as a charitable organization for Income Tax Exemption. Several people, including a lawyer, were certain we must be incorporated in order to qualify, and as this is an expensive and lengthy process. I could only pray that it would be unnecessary.

In September I received a reply asking for further information but giving no indication that we must incorporate. A lawyer friend arranged an appointment for me at the corporation branch of the Ontario Parliament Buildings. The head there was most cooperative and very sympathetic to our work, and on reading the letter from Ottawa, he seemed sure that incorporation would not be necessary. He thought, however, that I needed legal help with my reply to Ottawa and obtained an appointment with a lawyer who would do this without charge.

Together, we came up with a very legal looking document containing an analysis of our aims and the information requested. This I sent on to Ottawa. Miraculously, it worked, and contrary to the expectations of many, our registration came through shortly after we opened office. That was a happy day for Birthright! Since then, I have found that rarely is exemption given without corporation as a charitable, non-profit organization. The Spirit must have influenced our case.

Our present expenses now include rent but I hope that other centres will be as fortunate as we in finding free office space at first. Because we always consider the donation of our first office as our first major miracle, I think I should tell you about it.

In June of 1968, one of my little girls was hit by a car on her way to school, and, although not gravely injured, she did require minor surgery, and considerable post-operative care. The doctor's office was in a new modern building not far from the hospital, or from my own home.

On the day that I took her for her last appointment, I stood outside the tall building and glanced up at the sign, "Office Space for Rent." Less than two blocks away was the subway entrance and I thought: "If only I could obtain an office here!" For several months I had tried to find free office space without success. I took out a pen and old envelope from my purse and started to write down the telephone number from the sign. Suddenly a stranger spoke to me: "Madam, are you looking for an office?"

"Oh Yes," I replied, "but I have no money to pay for it."

"What do you want it for?"

"I want to start a centre to give help to distressed pregnant girls."

"Do you believe in the Lord?"

"Oh yes, of course."

"Do you believe in Jesus Christ and that He died for us?"

"Oh, of course, I believe that."

"Then I will give you an office free."

That was my introduction to Mr. J.D. Newfield, a devout Baptist, and wonderful Christian. When I climbed into my car and drove home, the tears were streaming down my cheeks. I believed that I had just seen God, and, indeed I know I *had* seen His intervention in the affairs of Birthright. In a moment of truth, I knew that Birthright was definitely in the divine plan of God, and that I was just a small instrument He was using to do His work. By a profession of faith in Him, and His divinity, Birthright became possible.

In early October I received about four hundred dollars in donations from some Roman Catholic clergy. The telephone account would be well over $50 a month which paid for two telephones and a tape recording to answer during "off" hours. Considering this, we really started on a "shoestring" and a prayer, and there was no money for advertising, except occasionally in the personal columns.

However, I do not hesitate to ask for donations, even though I know the Lord is providing. The money comes in, not a great deal at a time, but enough to meet expenses. A letter or a phone call is all that is needed to bring financial help.

Now, however, because of the way we have grown, and the demands made upon us, we are driving hard to obtain permanent yearly recants. Birthright here has reached the point where it is no longer possible to operate efficiently entirely on voluntary help. The demands made on my time by people all over the continent, in correspondence, is tremendous. Our own operation runs smoothly with our core group of women, highly efficient. We have high hopes of soon having a house as headquarters with adequate counselling rooms and emergency shelter for pregnant girls.

Many in the community are seeing our need, not only for office space and emergency shelter for our local needs, but also for international business. Public conscience requires that we grow and our needs be met. Babies' lives in Albuquerque, or Anchorage, or in far away New Zealand are as important to me as our own Canadian babies. Soon an international fund-raising plan may be put into effect and be repeated as the need arises. We ask all who uphold the sacredness of life to give, when Birthright calls on you, your dollar, for life. Give to your local Birthright office or to International Birthright.

Yet even as I speak like this, I ask understanding of my vision of Birthright. We are not a democratic organization, and must attempt, at all times, to prevent a structure which can hinder, rather than help, our work. Structure means politics, and when people begin to lobby for power or position, the Spirit is lost. It would seem that groups of deeply spiritual people working together in love and harmony, making every effort to make their own centres as effective as possible, will have little time for state and provincial meetings. Communication with other centres for purposes of exchange of ideas, and for reciprocal services, is readily possible by telephone. In time, a continental telephone "lifeline" may become a reality. God does not ask the impossible. It is true that there are people who would like more committees and meetings. I pray to God that this never happens, that international Birthright will never become a highly structured, bureaucratic international agency. If that should ever happen, the sensitive, person-to-person nature of our work will disappear, volunteers will leave, and the true spirit of Birthright will vanish from the earth. Our mission will have ended.

So, even as I appeal for the funds we need to be most effective, I do not by any means, mean to make us more technical. God forbid! I ask help to make possible the saving of more lives.

Last of all, I must pass on to you the advice once given to me by my very dear old friend, Mother Margarita, a Loretto sister, now over 90 years of age: "Dear, remember one thing. When you are doing the Lord's work He never gives you more than you need."

13. CONCLUSION

As I write this, Birthright is now over four years old and yet we have given some type of help to thousands of girls and women thus saving thousands of lives. This is only a beginning and we will go on to even greater things. Like St. Paul, we say: "Not that I have already obtained this or am already perfect; but I press on to make it my own, because Christ Jesus has made me His own; but one thing I do, forgetting what lies behind, and straining forward to what lies ahead, I press on towards the goal…, let us hold true to what we have attained." (Philippians 3: 12-16)

What I have most earnestly tried to convey to you is not only the details of the Birthright program, but also the approach which it embodies. I believe that this approach can be applied to every aspect of the abortion problem. We are in the realm of values and, as in the case with all of us in our care judgments about life, my approach is, in the final analysis, based on a set of moral principles. However, I am not just interested in defending my basic moral principles, but rather in showing that there is a source of practical ideas, of answers to human tragedy, and that they work.

Most babies are unwanted because their mothers are realistic and think that they cannot offer a decent life for their children. In reality, it is not the mother who decides that the child is not wanted but rather the society in which we live which labels the child "unwanted."

As I have said before, when a girl or woman cannot face the birth of her child gladly and joyfully because she has problems far beyond her capacity to solve, she should be able to trust in the community to surround and support her, to provide the assistance she needs. Today, we look to abortion as a means of helping the single pregnant girl and so we lose our sense of values and principles. It seems that our generation is so selfish and self-centred that it will not make sacrifices for tomorrow's generation. This is indeed a very great tragedy.

In Birthright we help rather than abort and are, indeed, proving that abortion need not be the way of the future. Again, I am compelled to say that there are other ways to cope with the problems we face, and these ways are preferable, not because they are quicker and easier, but because they show respect for human beings as they really are.

Love is the most needed ingredient in solving the problems of abortion. I do not speak here of a short-order sentimentality or of a "wishy-washy" love, but of an understanding, realistic love. It is not a question of money. If this were true, Birthright would never have gotten off the ground. Four years after opening, we are still just keeping ahead of the monthly bills. The question is whether our values are firm enough and our compassion strong enough. Too, sometimes just a soft word at the right moment, said in charity, wisdom and with a high level of common sense, can hold a world of charm against misery and pain.

Two years ago, on a Friday morning, a seventeen-year-old girl, Candy, six months pregnant, used her last dime to phone Birthright. She had nowhere to go and no prospect of a bed to sleep in that night. Through misunderstanding on her part of the Catholic Children's Aid Society to whom I referred her, by 9:30 p.m. she was still without help. I appealed to Larry Wilson of CHUM Radio, and he took her home for the weekend. On Monday, I took her to the Children's Aid, giving her my phone number. "Remember, honey, we're with you all the way and this dollar is for phone calls, to me, when you need me."

That night I had to drive her to the Emergency of a nearby hospital. She had tried to kill herself. She was in pain and deep depression. For three weeks she lay in hospital, under psychiatric care, and I went as often as possible to see her. She would talk to no one but me, because she knew I loved her. As one doctor put it, "This poor kid's been kicked out of here and there and now she doesn't want to live any longer."

But Candy lives and so does her child, because of Birthright. Early in her pregnancy she twice attempted to abort herself. This case has brought home to me, more than ever, how much needed we are in the community. Although basically our aim is the saving and preserving of human life, yet, by so doing, we are bringing love and therapy to hundreds. Girls like Candy are in every large city. Society in general does not accept the unwed mother and when a girl becomes pregnant, knowing full well that what happened to Candy could happen to her, she will take steps to rid herself of the pregnancy.

Birthright offers security and the knowledge that we exist will, very often, prevent a girl from seeking an abortion even if she delays coming to us until later in her pregnancy. That is why we cannot let her down.

People have asked me if I, personally, have experienced unwed motherhood since I seem to understand the girls so well. I have not had this experience, but I think I know what pain and suffering, heartache and despair are. I, too, know fears of the future, and many times I have come through a real crisis as to whether or not I am the person to continue directing Birthright. The demands of my family, my home, are many times in conflict with the needs of the girls, causing me great distress. As wonderful as the volunteers and clergy are in their support of me, the final decision, whether or not to continue, must come from me, and many times I quail inwardly as the future looms dark and fearful.

Then, suddenly, clearly, I am able to see that God is asking of me, not just faith in His word, but a readiness to trust myself to Him. Always, once again the pathway opens up for me as I read in Psalm 90: "You shall not fear the terror of the night, nor the arrow that flies by day, nor the pestilence that roams in the darkness, nor the devastating plague at noon. Though a thousand fall at your side, ten thousand at your right side, near you it shall not come."

With God's help, once again, I am able to continue.

I am nearing the end of this story, a story which gives, in reality, only brief idea of our work. Hundreds of such stories, full of sorrow turned to joy, are contained in the files of the founding office here and hundreds more are known in Birthright chapters from coast to coast. My days now are filled with the problems of directing a large international movement. There are those who, as in the beginning, see me as incompetent and inadequate. If I were alone, this would, of course, be true, but the Lord is with me, in all that I do as He is with the hundreds of dedicated Birthright people throughout the continent, as long as they rely on Him. Until God shows me otherwise, I must continue to guide the people of Birthright, on an international level. The abortion dilemma knows no boundary lines.

Some, unfortunately, do not have the true vision of Birthright, as being simply a pregnancy service. They would introduce family planning as part of the program. That is another area, even if related, and it is not the function of Birthright. Others are Catholic in name and service. How

erroneous this is! It is to be hoped they see that this must not happen, and how much it limits the scope of our work. Most girls of other faiths will not call a Birthright operating in Catholic Charities offices, nor will many Catholic girls. All of this has to change when funds permit the proper supervision of all the chapters. "Birthright" is not a name to be taken freely and lightly by any without permission, to give whatever type of service seems convenient. The number of officially chartered members is growing, and, united in a common aim and purpose, we will be firm in maintaining the standards of operation outlined in our Service Mark registration. No, Birthright is not a name. It is a concept.

There are a few who would destroy us, who have tried to gain control in the past, without success. With funds and time on their side, they do everything possible to bring Birthright under their jurisdiction. But this can never be because I know so very well now that:

"The Lord is my shepherd, I shall not want; he makes me lie down in green pastures. He leads me beside still waters; he restores my soul. He leads me in paths of righteousness for his name's sake. Even though I walk through the valley of the shadow of death, I fear no evil; for thou art with me; thy rod and thy staff they comfort me. Thou preparest a table before me in the presence of my enemies; thou anointest my head with oil, my cup runneth over. Surely goodness and mercy shall follow me all the days of my life; and I shall dwell in the house of the Lord forever." (Psalm 23)

Abortion is being used now as an explosive political weapon but legislators should keep in mind that it is a two-edged sword. We should keep in mind that, along with all the unwanted people who will die, thousands of very much wanted babies, future citizens of our countries, will also die. Are there now any unwanted babies? Thousands of childless couples are now

anguished. There are almost no babies to adopt. Can we say babies are unwanted?

It takes a special quality to be willing to suffer to give life but, as the Lord said, "He who loses his life shall find life."

Let us organize our lives around the supreme value, that God is the creator of life, and He alone has the right to take life.

"And surely your blood of your lives will I require, at the hand of every beast will I require it, and at the hand of man, and at the hand of every man's brother will I require the life of man. Whoso sheddeth man's blood, by man shall his blood be shed: for in the image of God, made He man." (Genesis 9: 5, 6)

What does the future hold for Birthright? Only God can know this – but like Abraham we will venture forth and go where God leads us. Let us hope it will be into every city in North America, and some day, perhaps, all around the world.